BREAKING EVEN

(Punching trauma in its face
while staying calm,
cool,
and
completely weird.)

a memoir by Simone Le Ann

There was a dream I had a few months ago, it trapped me in a world that I already was so familiar with. It was in the house I grew up in. The one with the paint chipping away from the red front door that revealed the old wood underneath. It was just as I remembered it. I walked up the poorly carpeted wooden stairs to the pepto bismol pink bathroom. I saw my mother standing right there in the hallway. Her bedroom was at the far end of the hallway, she may have just woken up because she was still in her nightgown. Although, if you knew her well enough you know very well that she lived in her "moo moos". It was her off white and powder blue, sleeveless nightgown. The one with the forget-me-nots embroidered across her chest with pink roses intertwined. It appeared as if she was almost floating to me. She seemed so peaceful. Flowing, her nightgown had a halo of a glow just as her skin did. She gently brushed back my hair behind my right ear and asked if I had forgotten her. I told her that there was no way in hell that I would have ever forgotten her, that I loved and missed her very much. She smiled her martyr smile and told me that she loved me too and at the moment, I was shaken awake by my husband and my children.

They had been yelling my name for many minutes. I was so far away in the familiar home with my mom that I just couldn't hear them. Perhaps I just chose not to, perhaps I just wanted to stay a little longer with my mom? Just a bit longer to look at her smile. My husband had to physically shake my shoulders to wake me up that morning. I don't think I was dreaming though. I was just somewhere else in that house, the house I grew up in, with my mom. Everything was the same, I was home and never before had I felt so alone.

Every single night I find myself wide awake around the same time of day. It's either early morning or late night. Either way you look at it, I shouldn't be awake at this hour. My clammy skin is soaking wet and cold from the sweat I am drenched head to toe in. I'm constantly fighting my memories in my panicky PTSD caused fits. I've already changed my pajamas twice. I can feel that the pillow between my legs is now also wet and wrinkled as I roll over in an attempt to shake my body and pillow free of the nightmares. I drag my aching legs to the bathroom and press my face against the cold window to bring myself back to the "now."

My sleeping life is always my past life, and "she" is always there. Always the same. My mom is always there, even as I would roll my eyes and hold the phone a foot away from my head nodding and rolling my eyes. She is still there every night in her haunting fashion. Only now, I cannot text her and tell her what she did in my dream. Only now, I have to feel her life and her death every single day to remind myself that she is no longer here with me.

Today, I am in our living room and my children are upstairs. Each is in their own room having "quiet time" after lunch, my husband reads and I sit here writing. I slip away into thought. When I was my oldest son's age, I remember having to get a butter knife from the kitchen to scrape the crust from inside of my underwear to have a semi clean pair for primary school. It was too caked on, and my shitty nails were just not cutting it, literally. My mom was probably lightly boozed and slightly hungover in between boyfriends and jobs, often. She didn't have time to do our laundry at the laundromat that was just a few buildings down from our low-income apartment. It's okay though, because we made do, and she worked her ass off to provide. Today I make sure that my children have clean laundry every single day. Even if that means that I have to skip game night with the family or stay up later than everyone else. I spend many hours of the week washing, drying, separating, folding, and repeating.

We had ringworm as kids, I think that is when other people began noticing the filth we had become accustomed to. I used to think it meant that there were tons of tiny worms living in my skin and that maybe I could be the star of a sci-fi film! I had always wanted to be in the movies so here was my chance as some weird, freaky, freckle faced nobody with worms crawling under their skin. Neat!

She comes home and yells,
As we all fall apart,
The hatred in the walls,
The blackness in our hearts,
The walls are screaming,
Pain is a permanent feeling,
How can I tell you,
Just how scared we are,
Hateful thoughts will leave you alone,
Greedy for more,
But it was always right in front of you,
Sitting on the dining room table,

Waiting for you to reach for more,
Seconds, minutes pass now,
An hour is too long to wait for an apology,
I look forward to your eulogy,
Sort of perfect in nearly every way,
It's just another promise, something you'll
never say.

My husband likes to remind me that the kids made the mess and therefore, they can clean up themselves. I really do have a problem with that. He asks me, "didn't you ever have to clean your room as a kid?" No sir, I did not. Not because we had a butler or because my mommy would always do it for me, but because my mom was never really that strict about it to be honest. I can remember sharing a room with my sister and under our day beds we would have stored our week-old soda or kool-aid bottles growing mold, candy wrappers with chewed up candy still tucked inside with spit bubbles still intact, the occasional dust bunny or two, many, many crumbs, and apparently a condom? I heard there was a condom under my bed as a kid. Is it true? I have no idea and honestly it is not an area inside of myself that I care to tap into.

There was a day that I can remember very well when my sister and I were younger. Our grandmother came over to take us to have fun with her for the day. She walked into our bedroom and started sobbing. We were living in trash up to our ankles, but we truly didn't know any better because we were not taught any better. My mom was sick, she had an illness, she was not fully aware of her mental illnesses back then and we did not keep ourselves or our home clean because none of us fully knew how to.

My husband and I do not allow food upstairs, the only drink allowed upstairs is water. My children have snack times at 9 am and roughly 3 pm, downstairs, sometimes with cartoons and sometimes not. I will do better. I will be better.

I heard a rumble upstairs as I am the only one awake. I hope it was the cat. My husband and I have been married for a little over eight years now. He has changed my view on a lot of matters, not forcefully, but by helping show me with kindness and love. I have never met someone as wholesome as he is and I am so thankful for him. He has opened my eyes to the world that I had been blindly walking for 21 years. He showed me how to find the beauty in this place.

For so long before him I had been self medicating with practically any drug or drink I found to the point of floating in between reality and my own little fantasy land. Very early in 2010 I willingly checked myself into a mental health hospital. I had recently lost my job at a furniture store, the one that I was stealing money from, and I failed at going further as a contestant on a reality TV show in LA. My boyfriend at the time had just dumped me. I had to move back home after living in our apartment. My favorite grandmother had just passed away from complications due to her lupus, and the car that was in my mom's name was repossessed due to my failed payments.

The first time that I can remember trying to kill myself, I was 11 years old. We had this absolutely, wildly, adorable bathroom in the house that I grew up in. The bathroom walls were a pasty Pepto Bismol pink. The bathroom floor was tiled black and white like a checkerboard pattern. Against the wall that connected to my shared bedroom with my sister, was a claw foot bathtub. The tub itself was white and underneath was black. The faucets were copper and labeled "hot and cold" the knobs were rusty silver. I was given a white training bra that had been passed down to me from my big sister at the ripe old age of eleven. It may have been one of the days my sister chased me around the house with a butcher's knife as she did this a few times. I looped my training bra around the shower rod of the claw foot bathtub. Yes, I already know that I am a genius. I cried for a few minutes before I stepped onto the ledge of the bathtub and stuck my head through the white hole of the training bra straps. I jumped off the ledge of that claw foot bathtub and the shower rod came crashing down. My 100 pound, eleven year old chunky ass just sort of plopped down right there on the black and white checkered floor . I said to myself, "Well okay then," and I carried on with my day. I got dressed and then skipped over to the neighbor's house with my apple juice box in hand to play with my friend's poly pockets. She had the absolute best collection I had ever seen and really, I am still envious of her collection.

The second time that I attempted suicide was on New Year's Day 2010. My closest friends and I snuck three bottles of wine from one of their father's New Year's parties in the basement of the house, one for each of us underage girls. We truly thought that we were so clever. The other two girls danced, and sang, and celebrated the new year chiming in on the grandfather clock as the adults in the basement drunkenly celebrated. I downed my own personal bottle of wine in a matter of minutes and then drove myself home. Continuing on my downward spiral I crept my bony fingers inside the communal medicine cabinet. I quickly downed my 30 count of a freshly refilled bottle of Wellbutrin with a gulp of rail vodka and orange juice. A few hours later I stumbled into my mom's bedroom clenching my chest.

Something felt funny and I was quick to tell my mom that something was wrong. It was tight and fluttering, like a butterfly under a plastic film, stretched too thin to flutter correctly. She was so pissed off that I woke her up in the middle of the night. I collapsed on her floor and had a seizure. My mom called an ambulance and the paramedics arrived quickly and cut open my favorite red and black checkered dress that I had just recently thrifted. So then at that point, I too was pissed off. The paramedics were doing their best to keep me awake in the back of the ambulance and I was taken to the nearest hospital where I underwent evaluations and two days later, I officially woke up and I was diagnosed with bipolar depression.

Last night my husband and I toasted our sparkling grape juice and kissed at 8 pm after putting our kids to bed and then I took my congested, thirty year old, chunky ass, and plopped right into our king sized bed.

Happy fucking New Years.

Is it the paranoia, or the pills
Either way I've had my fill,
Not on fuel and not on sleep,
But on the secrets, I silently keep,
Keeping time is no concern,
Lost the concept, lost my turn,
Losing weight and gaining bone,
Loner Wolf is all alone,
I cannot hold onto a moment,
As miniscule as sand,
Slips through my translucent skin,

And burns into my hand,
Seeping into the bloodstream,
The clots continue to grow,
Inching further every moment,
Down, Down, Down,
Down my neck,
Down my spine,
Drown me out,
In a bottle of wine.

Please do not think that my mom was just a horrible person. She was a little bit of a horrible person, but I truly do not think that she knew how to help it. I did not understand it when I was young, I did not even understand it until after her accident. I know now that she was ill. My mom was silently mentally ill, and she did not know it for most of her life. She was born in the 60's and as a Baby Boomer, mental health is not an important issue. It is rarely talked about. The "hush hush" society of the self-medicated, overworked and underpaid, blue-collar drones of America.

I remember crawling into the backseat of our shitty four door sedan after a "daddy weekend", spent in his trailer with his wife and their son. I had to shuffle around some empty beer cans to lay down on the smokey interior so I could rest my eyes but the smells of her previous night were making me nauseous, and she told me to grab an empty McDonalds cup to barf in and so I did. I had a really hard time sleeping at my dad's house. Everything in his home was a complete 180 rotation of life at my mom's house. At my dad's house, my sister and I had clean clothes, clean sheets, warm meals together as a family at a table, bedtime stories and silly songs. It was almost as if when I was at my dad's house I was in a dream world, and living with my mom was a living, breathing, nightmare. I grew up as Two Face. I had a fairytale life with my dad, and hell on Earth at times with my mom. It was not entirely her fault though. She really loved me and she loved me a lot I think.

Life with my dad was full of laughter and sunshine and many, many unfamiliar faces. My dad met a woman at a bar that his band was performing at shortly after my parents divorced when I was maybe three years old. His girlfriend quickly became pregnant and from there, she quickly became his wife and the three became a family. My dad had a new girl, he also had a brand-new baby on the way, a whole new family before I was three years old. Here, everything that I thought was my normalcy was ripped from right underneath me. I was four years old when my brother was born and every other weekend, we were able to be a family for a few hours.

My dad has been a drummer in local bands ever since I can remember. He has been playing the drums since he was young, and he is very good at what he does. Friday nights at his house were usually spent together watching a Friday night lineup and eating crappy store brand pizza. We loved it. On Saturday night's my dad usually had to go play music in his band so we had a babysitter from 5 pm onward into the early hours of the following morning. Sunday morning after breakfast, it was time to go back with our mom. I was able to spend time with my father for approximately 40 hours per month aside from the occasional holiday and I still hope to learn who this man is. I have always loved my dad but I don't know anything about him other than what his social media accounts portray.

The truth is, I have never felt welcomed in my stepmother and father's home. They had their beautiful older daughter, they had their younger son, they had an obnoxious piece of the puzzle that did not fit and sounded and looked just like her mother. Simone is her mother, Simone is sassy. Simone talks back. No, Simone is just, and will do what she needs to do to bring justice to what is in front of her. Maybe it's the Libra in me. Maybe it's because I am just like mom.

My stepmother's family has never accepted me as their family and this is why I have also not accepted them. My father has always been there to stick up for his wife even through the beginning when she was cheating on him. He has his daughter, he has his son, he has his wife. There is no use and no space for me in his life and there never has been. My parents were divorced before I was even two years old and less than two years later, I was replaced. For so long I have felt the bottomless floor of displacement and rejection from the people I want to love so badly, though I am kept out. I forgive myself for trying to love humans that are incapable of loving me back and I will let go of the grievance that this has plagued me with.

I was 11 years old and on the cusp of 12 when my mom first threatened me with death. It sounds way worse than it was, I think. My mom was driving her red Jeep Liberty with the windows down as it was summertime, the radio was on, and we were passing familiar streets when I encouraged the subject of moving in to live at my dad's house. My sister was already living with him, and I so badly wanted to be with her. She was a perfect person in my eyes. She was the one who protected me when I needed her and was there to speak for me when I could not speak. I wanted to live with her because I missed her just so fucking much. My two-year-old brother was in the front seat, no, not legal, but he was buckled so maybe that counts? My mom turned the radio off and with no warning she accelerated from 25mph to nearly 60mph on a side street adjacent to the street I grew up on. I threw both of my arms around my baby brother in the front seat. Her voice was hoarse and raised, she was screaming through her teeth as she often did at this point. "If you don't live with me, you don't live at all, got it?" I was crying and begging. I wanted to live, even if this was the living that was going to be lived. I still chose life. So, I stayed with my abuser for just a few more years before moving to my dad's house for just a few more years too.

I can only stay for a little bit at a time before I end up fucking up somehow. My sister had by then moved back to my mom's place at the time I went to live with my dad, and I had hoped for her too. I do not know why she did not like me, but I so badly wanted to be just like her. I loved her so much.

As I sit here in my home listening to my three children playing downstairs with their daddy, I am so grateful for what we have built. Rising from raising ourselves to raising children of my own, I am so thankful I am still here. I am still trying to find my religious footing in this world, but I catch myself asking God why I am still here. I do not deserve to be. I have not been a good person my whole life. I have not helped the homeless every Sunday or donated the clothes off my back to keep a sick animal warm. I am human and I am trying. That really is my only goal for this book, and for whomever decides to read this, I want you to know that no matter what your past, present, and incredible debt, you can still rise above these mountains and continue the climb. You can still fight. I am relentless and you are too, we have to just try. I am making these pledges and promises right there with you. I know that I can be capable of so much more than what I was grown up to believe. I have let most of my life play on a reel right in front of me and without blinking I have never gotten up to stop the rolling film.

I am so tired.
Yet I am so wired,
To climb.

I must give my mom some credit for being there for me. That is what moms are biologically programmed to do! Through every surgery I had as a child, every heartbreak I had as a teenager and into adulthood, she was there for all of the bad times, and she was there for the best times. She encouraged me to pursue whatever it was in this world that would make my heart happy. When I thought I could be a pilot, she bought me a private lesson with a pilot at our local airport. When I wanted to be a writer, she encouraged my writing by purchasing me notebooks and even printing some of my childhood work. When I wanted to be a model, even though I am hardly even 5'6" anymore, she supported me. She was not herself when she was yelling in my face until her teeth were grinding, her nostrils were flaring, and her face was burning a steamy red. She was not herself when she would call me a bitch occasionally, or tell me I was an unfit mother. She was not herself when she called me a slut and asked who I'd be fucking that day because every day it was someone new apparently, even though I can count on two hands the number of men and women I have slept with. She was not herself when she had me backed into a corner in the kitchen of our childhood home slapping my face back and forth with both sides of her hands. I don't even remember why, probably because I talked back. I am sometimes mouthy. I am not sure that I really knew who she was. Some days were super fun surprise school pick-ups from elementary school and gifts like the Tamagotchi keychain pets. Unfortunately though, for every happy day in the family room with the sun shining on our faces as we try out the newest food, a Lunchables for the very first time, there were double the amount of days that I would cry myself to sleep from hunger, or from the pain she physically or mentally inflicted into by dumb malformed brain.

I waited and waited and waited for her to wake up. I was about five years old, and it was well into a Saturday morning. My stomach had been rumbling for hours but I didn't know quite how to make my own food. My mom was sleeping off her hangover with whoever her one night stand was in the evening prior. I figured the only way I was going to stop those loud hunger growls was to make myself breakfast. We never had much food wise as a kid, I pretty much grew up on slim jims and oodles of noodles. Again, I have no idea how I'm still here. So, I went to the refrigerator and focused my tired eyes around the shelves to see what on Earth I could possibly make. I decided a sandwich would be the easiest choice. I took out two slightly green slices of bread, maybe it's a new kind of bread she bought that she just forgot to tell us about. I grabbed every condiment I could see. People put condiments on sandwiches I thought. Jelly, mustard, mayonnaise, ketchup, pickles, chocolate syrup, oh yeah, and cheese! I proudly stacked my sandwich almost too tall for my tiny mouth and sat down on the kitchen floor to eat my masterpiece. I was nearly halfway through my condiment sandwich before I ran to the toilet and vomited. Well at least my stomach didn't hurt anymore I thought.

I was fifteen years old when I started to watch my weight. Looking back, I don't think at all that I was a chubby girl and it still pisses me off that I ever did. I was fifteen years old when my stepmother stopped me in my bedroom door frame and told me to cover up my gut before leaving the house. My stupid fucking gut. I counted calories in my sophomore year of high school. I would also try to move my body as much as I physically could to stay active. It wasn't until I was sixteen before I discovered my love-hate relationship with eating disorders. I started dating a boy when I was sixteen, my first "real" boyfriend I suppose. One of his roommates at the time had joked about which one of us wore the bigger sized girl jeans and I know that it was me, my own dad pointed out to me when I was fifteen that I had "childbearing hips." I grew up believing I was a big, fat , woman just like "your mother." That really stuck with me, I still think about those words every day, that and covering up my gut. I would only eat a blow pop and a diet coke for lunch in junior year of high school and all the way through to my senior year of high school. I looked forward to the day that I didn't have to sit through classes and cafeterias surrounded by carbs and calories I wouldn't ever touch.

Breakfast wasn't ever on my mind and honestly, I still struggle to eat breakfast today. I have learned how to nourish and take care of my body throughout the years, but I am still working on my relationship with breakfast. When I wasn't starving myself, I was binging and purging. It literally was a high for me. I would spend entire paychecks working at The Gap outlet store, and the day was spent buying pizzas, salads, onions rings, fries, and ice cream. I would sometimes spend an entire day bouncing between different restaurants and order whatever I wanted off of the menu in order to have control, to binge and purge. To feel it and then to vomit it back up was my one and only control in my life. I could do this thing where I could eat whatever I wanted and I wouldn't gain weight, how lucky am I to find this method I thought.

There was a time when I was working a double shift as a hostess at a restaurant that I thought I might actually die if I didn't make myself purge. I was so hungry that day from working such long hours. At the end of my final shift that day I had a huge binge session at the restaurant. There were still customers in the restroom and when they left, employees came in. If I didn't throw up soon, I felt like my heart was going to explode or I would gain ten pounds or probably both. After getting in my car, I made a few phone calls to a few local pharmacies and lied about having a child who consumed poison, therefore I would need an IPECAC so that I could administer the medication and my fake child could throw up the fake poison. I have the voice of a twelve-year-old girl, they knew that I was lying. I never did get a chance to purge, instead I just went home and went to bed, and I slept so well that night.

Bulimia never crossed my mind until it did. Then it didn't leave my mind for almost an entire decade. My brother and I shared the main bathroom, but it was mostly just his. The mirror above the bathroom sink was stained with toothpaste streaks and the mirror was broken in at least two different corners. The floor mats in front of the bathroom sink and the toilet in the bathroom were always slightly damp with urine from my brother not knowing or maybe just not trying to aim his stream at all. The toilet itself was a porcelain biohazard. Vomit was caked onto the floor surrounding the toilet and along the bottom sides of the toilet were stained rings of different shades of brown and yellow and sometimes blue because my brother drank a shit ton of Gatorade. There were never any hand towels or even any clean towels to use after a shower, I usually had one towel to clean myself up after binging and one for showering. I'm not sure that the shower and tub combo my brother and I shared had ever even been cleaned once while we lived there. When my brother was using the bathroom and I had just finished a binging episode I would just stay in my room to vomit. I'd collect Tupperware or pots or pans from the kitchen and head back to my room with some water. I would forcefully vomit into these different bowls and pans and if I could not get to the bathroom to flush it down, I would just hide it and let it sit until the next binging session and it was full. I found it easy to vomit when the bowl was giving off an odor that would make anyone gag. Once the vomit bucket was full and no one was home, I would lift the heavy container and carry the jiggling chunks to our main bathroom and dump the vomit soup into the toilet. Occasionally this would cause the toilet to clog, but I always knew how to fix it.

My husband recently helped me get dental

insurance a few weeks ago. I am missing 4-5 teeth from my love-hate relationship with my eating disorder. I don't like to smile for photos because I am embarrassed of what I have done to myself. I am truly grotesque in my eyes. I went years under the radar with my eating disorder, under the radar and underweight. It wasn't until I was pregnant with my first child that I realized that I needed help. Never have I been hospitalized for my ED, but instead I have slowly retaught myself the importance of food and feeding yourself is so important to feeling well and being well in general. I love food now. I can honestly say that I do not have any aspects of my eating disorder anymore. There are days I will daydream and think oh well, I know the easy way to get that bikini body. Fuck the easy way out. I am not a coward. If there's anything my mom has taught me, it is to not be a coward, well that and how to drive after drinking way too much. Honestly her technique helped me drive from drinking a solo bottle of wine on New Year's Day 2010 to getting home safely and taking a bottle of pills to try to end my life apparently. But hey, I did get home safely, so there is that. Thanks mom.

This past year after losing my mom due to complications from a freak, tragic, accident has left me feeling so changed. Not necessarily in a "woke" sense, I just feel that I am more alive. I can walk outside and lift my face to the cold wind, and she is embracing me with her arms and holding me so tight in the cold air. I take photos of my children and in the sunrays, I can see her face. Often, I wonder if she knew if I loved her enough because I really, really did. I kept my kids away from her house because she was a very heavy smoker. I grew up in it and I didn't want my children to even spend one night in that. I also was afraid of her anger outbursts. At this point I am an adult with my own family, so I am not around her much, does she still have them? Will she put a knife to her wrist and tell my children the same thing she said to me, "you make me want to do this every single day." I couldn't live with myself if I knowingly exposed them to the same toxins, I have been trying to rid myself of the past thirty years. I was twenty-one years old and had just started dating my now husband. My mom and I had gotten into an argument about what I have no idea about, after going to my bedroom and shutting the door, she had come in with a knife to her wrist telling me that every day she wants to kill herself because of me. That night I took all of the knives out of their spot in the kitchen drawer and safely wrapped them up in a towel and hid them away, high up in my closet on a shelf. When she had her accident seven years later, I would be the one that would have to scrub the carpet of her newly purchased home in an attempt to clean the blood stains. Why is her blood always on my hands? I failed at that too as the stain only lightened a few shades to a pastel pink.

She had an accident in her workplace early in

the 2000s. With medical help she was able to be seen by the nearby hospital and they came to the conclusion she had a herniated disk in her back. Many years and surgeries and procedures passed before she was granted disability for her incident at her workplace. Her employer did not pay for her to have a worker's comp as they stated. She was technically not working at the time of the accident, instead what happened was that she was walking up the stairs to clock in for the day. After finally receiving her settlement, she was approved for a loan to purchase a home. There were many different rules within the fine lines of buying a home with disability money. Basically, the best house she could get in her budget was over an hour away in Cumberland, Maryland. We were hesitant to see her move that far from us because we have always been a fifteen-minute drive away at the most. I know that to many families, being an hour away is nothing, but we have always been close to her so the idea of her being over an hour away made us feel uneasy. My mom and I have also butted heads our entire relationship as I now see because I am so much like her. I have to admit I was a little bit looking forward to her moving an hour away, it was a good amount of distance for us to not drive each other up the wall. That stupid Cumberland house.

It had only been three days, roughly 72 hours after signing the paperwork and receiving the keys to her home, that she had her accident. There was a documentary style show on Netflix called,

"The Staircase" about a well-off family and a drunk accident on a staircase. We are not and have never been a well-off family. It was never investigated, and that part still haunts me. My mom was found in a puddle of her own blood six hours after she had fallen headfirst down her wooden attic stairs butt naked. She was in and out of consciousness listening to her favorite pro baseball team play on the tv in her bedroom just a few feet from where she landed until she was found by my half-brother who was living in the basement at the time with his girlfriend. His girlfriend was supposedly at the house, in the basement the entire time my mom was bleeding out of her skull. My brother was apparently working during the day of her accident. My mom stated that she was trying to move boxes that my brother was supposed to move to the attic, but he just didn't get around to it, when she fell down the old wooden attic steps that had no railing on either side. I get it, life gets in the way. I spoke to her on the phone that morning as I was still on the fence about whether or not an abortion was the best option for my growing zygote. She annoyed me with her wisdom, and I rolled my eyes at her knowledge as I often did. I told her I would call her back later on after I had time to clean up my kid's breakfast mess. I never called her back that day because life often gets in the way. When she was found six hours after her life-threatening injury, she tried to tell my sister that it was kind of a funny story about how it happened. We had so many questions then. We still have so many questions. My brother wasn't speaking to me (still isn't,) and he didn't want to clean the bloody mess that was stained into the carpet now. My sister walked me through the house that my mom had just signed the papers on a few days before. It was my first time ever standing there in the home that my mom was so excited about. She planned for her grandchildren to stay the night at Nana's and go for a hike on the nearby path. Instead, I hiked up the old carpeted stairs and used every chemical in the house that I could find to scrub the outdated blue carpet as her black lab, a dog she had since a puppy that she named Lola came over very excitedly and licked my nose.

Instead of an investigation, the local fire department had to haul my mother out of her spare bedroom window down to the ambulance because her home was too old, and the walls were too narrow for an ambulance gurney to fit. That stupid Cumberland house. I didn't get the call until I had already climbed into bed for the night. My sister texted my phone, but I was already asleep, she then called me, but my phone was on silent. My husband woke me up and told me that my sister had been trying to get a hold of me because our mom had an accident. I had no expectations on what shape she was in. All I knew was that she had fallen and was rushed to the hospital by ambulance. The hospital she was originally taken to was not well equipped to take care of a spinal cord injury patient and the weather conditions were too poor for a helicopter ride. So, she was then taken to a hospital well over two hours away by ambulance and we were finally able to go see her two days after her accident. Maybe if she was flown, they could have done something to save her sooner but the fact is, she had now been almost twelve hours past her accident, it was too late to fix all of the damage.

The very first memory I have of my mom is of her smiling her very contagious smile. Perhaps it's really just a staged JCPenney photo that I remember, but to be quite honest with you, my memory is shit. It's definitely at least somewhat from being an undiagnosed alcoholic or self-medicating with cannabis but yeah, I can barely remember what I had to eat today. My mom also had a shit memory, it got much worse and became much more apparent in her later years. She didn't come to my first child's baby shower because she said she had anxiety and was apparently about to have a panic attack once she arrived at the location of the baby shower. This was new. It was 2012 when she finally admitted that she may be having some real mental health issues. I was pretty devastated when she came for the five minutes to my baby shower to tell me that she wasn't actually going to come in. I should have known better. I grew up on her broken promises, so I just brushed it off and smiled through the pain like I always did. As kids she promised me and my siblings a lot of things. One thing in particular that she would always promise to me was to take me skiing.

She had promised me we would go skiing when I was a kid and to this day I still haven't gone. Maybe next year. It was always "Maybe next year." Maybe I held on to the promise too hard, my expectations were set way too high. I dreamed of zipping down a steep mountain but next year was never the year. Or the year after that or that one and so on and so on, perhaps I'll take the ⅓ bag of her ashes down the slopes someday.

Penny pinching wishes,
On secondhand dishes,
One, two, tie your shoe,
Each day is a blur,
And then you're four,
And five,
And somehow, you're still alive,
On this spinning rock,
Taking everything for granted,
Even the granite.

We do not encourage promises or expectations in our home. That sounds a little sad I can understand, but also, we are teaching our children to not hold their hopes and expectations too high because that fall down really fucking hurts. I was not born with a silver spoon in my mouth but rather a plastic spork. I felt quite disposable most of my life and especially when I started to date my first boyfriend. We began dating when I was sixteen and the summer to follow, he broke up with me to have a "break." Wow, I was a dummy. If you don't know this, a break is code for fucking other people, but still staying loose on a tight rope because the other person will come back once they get bored of the flavor of the week. Stop. If it is a break, just break it off. I stayed on his leash of lust for nearly six years before I realized that I might not actually be disposable, and there might actually be a chance I could have real actual love. He told me once years later that the only reason he dated me was because I was a slut. Although he was my first and I thought he loved me and I loved him but I was so wrong. I was just a dumb, unwanted, unloved, slut. My mom and this boy seemed to be able to beat me down with the same cycling of words. That's what it is broken down to in the most simple form, a cycle. It became a cycle of break ups and makeups and reconnecting and disposing and ups and many, many heart breaks. My dearest mom was there for it all.

When I was younger the movie, "Matilda,"

SIMONELE ANN

came out to the theaters. I saw a knock off VHS but hey, still counts. Ms. Honey was everything I dreamed a mother would be. I had begged and pleaded with God to give me to a different family so many nights as a child. One that would love me and one that was as kind and patient as Ms. Honey was. I made a promise to myself when I married my husband that if we ever had children, then I would be Ms. Honey. Obviously, no one is quite as perfect as she is made out to be, but we certainly do try our best to raise good humans compassionately. So we don't live in a cute little cottage off a dirt road with gorgeous overgrown trees and a vibrant garden. So okay maybe I say fuck way too much in front of my kids, but I'm still compassionate about it. I never wanted to be that angry teeth grinding mother. A mother figure to me was lazy, tired, boozed, angry, overweight, unkind, and unpleasant. I promised myself I would never be like that. I will be better, I have to be better.

I must have been twelve or maybe thirteen when I had my first alcoholic beverage. My best friend growing up was the neighbor's daughter. Her parents were out shopping at the grocery store when she showed me where her parents hid their booze. We thought it was silly, we did a lot of bad things together that we thought were silly. So, we tasted her parents' various flavors of schnapps and after finishing a six pack of Slim Fasts we went down to the basement. Her basement was so strange to me, the layout, the strange smells of bacon, coffee, urine, and stale weed. It was my escape. Her basement was where I came alive, maybe for an hour or two. It was her that taught me I like girls as well as boys. If we moved our bodies together in a certain way, it felt nice, really, really, really nice. I was twelve I guess when I had my first orgasm with another human. I mean yeah, I have done the DIY method, but this, this was new. We were still living in our shitty section 8 apartment when I first stumbled upon my mother's sexual health interests. I found a stack of magazines under the far right side of her bed. Tons and tons of topless women doing things to each other and also to men, things I had never even thought of. I was interested.

I have never dated a woman, only men. However, I have had sex with another woman, just one. I am not sure that was the right choice for me. It was twisty and awkward and there were lots of knees and elbows flying around, very graceful I'm sure you can imagine. Admittingly, I have to say that I was very liquored up after snorting a line of crushed Vicodin. Excuses, excuses. The excuses held me back from ever really testing the waters with dating women because I was raised to think that was wrong in God's eyes. To this day I still find myself attractive to both men and women and I can actually say that with pride. My mom had a few best friends growing up, some I remember more than others. One in particular that sticks out was Holly. Tall, blue eyed, blonde hair, perfect smile, Holly. I think my mom may have liked her a little more than a friend, but we never talked about it. My mom was never too open about her love life, the pieces were all there, but putting the puzzle together wasn't her job. I do wish we could have openly talked about love, life, anger, mental health. We couldn't talk about sex, ever. We saw Titanic when it came to theaters and every nude scene my sister and I would dive to the popcorn bag at our feet and snicker. After intermission of the film I was very puzzled by Rose and her attempted suicide. I remember asking my mother why on Earth somebody would want to end their life, and all she said was, "you will someday." She was right.

I started to fear death at a very young age, I was three or four years old when my first close family death occurred. Often, I found myself daydreaming about an afterlife or lack thereof. Barely able to catch my breath and myself from thinking too many negative thoughts and spiraling into a childhood depression. The feelings still hit me today and I find that I can hardly breathe in fear of death and the end being such a sparkless event. I would be there in my day bed, the one that is stained and dirty, missing half of the much-needed screws to hold it together. One of the posts holding the bed frame in place that was elegantly painted white with a gold trim and pink roses, was broken. Inside the post I would stuff my trash so that mom wouldn't notice the heaps of garbage spread along the floor. I would take off the elegantly painted bulb on the post and shove down as many candy wrappers as I could fit before you'd start to see the crinkle of the plastic jolly rancher wrapper poking out. All four posts I did this to instead of walking my lazy ass to a trash can. That's another thing though, my mom's mental illness left our homes completely unclean. Every apartment, every duplex, every townhome, every house, filth.

One duplex owner actually took her to court in regards to her filth. I went to court with her and spoke to her privately about just paying the fines. I was twenty years old and I knew way better than to live like she had us living. It was easy to make yourself vomit when the bathroom had never been cleaned and urine stains were as far as the eye could see, including the ceiling. My mom had an issue with her bladder her entire life and when she worked two hours away, she would wear adult diapers to and from work because of the traffic she would often be caught in. The bathroom that was attached to her bedroom in the master had a collection of her piss filled adult diapers stacked almost as high as the bathroom window. She never was good at throwing things away and I can understand the hoarding from her depression or cleaning things up and that all could have been addressed and treated properly if only she was able to see her mental illness.

I still fear death and dying probably even more now that I have children of my own and have lost my mom at a relatively early age in life. I am afraid of the world outside of my front doorsteps and I fear I won't leave a mark for the future to see. The world we knew is currently frozen in time as we navigate our new normal during a global pandemic. I don't want to be just a photograph or a fuzzy memory in only my children's heads. In a love and feared relationship with the world has given me a permanent sense of hyperactivity which hinders my depression and accelerates my mania. My bipolar medication has increased in milligrams twice in the past four years and I am now one increase away from the max dose. The anti-anxiety medication I am prescribed from time to time is given when my panic attacks get ahead of me. Will I always be medicated, until the day I die? What are the long-term side effects of these medications vs what are the long term side effects if I don't continue this treatment plan. Without my medications I know that I am angry, suicidal, manic, depressed, and impulsive. I fear what my life would look like if I do not have access to these medications and a support team of help for my mental health. I fear what my life was before these medications. I will forgive myself for hosting these fears and somehow and in some way, I will forgive myself for who I was before I started to take control of my mental illnesses, please forgive me also. I am not myself when I am unmedicated.

As I sit here in my king-sized bed with a full tummy, the one bathroom we have is currently occupied by my husband giving our three children a bath. I yelled at them today and I feel so awful about it now. I took the two older children grocery shopping with me, okay first mistake. I let the two of them push their own child sized carts around the store, second mistake. After locking them in the car for their own safety and walking away to just take a deep breath alone, I had to catch myself. I will not be like her. I have to be better. I inhaled the cold January air and shuffled back to our Xterra. I was an asshole and I told them I was sorry for acting the way I did. My poor children were crying because they thought I was leaving them. My mom never apologized. It was almost as if the moment had never even happened. Apologies came too short and acknowledgement was much shorter.I have become accustomed to walking away from my problems when the going gets too tough for me to handle. These are my children and I abandoned them in their eyes. Truly all I did was walk around the corner of the grocery store building to take a deep breath but to them I left. I feel sick just thinking about it. I am her. I am building their memories on abandonment and rage just as I grew to know her and myself and my surroundings. Thankfully I know when I need to control myself, I will be better. I have to be.

I have been on Zoloft for nearly 4 years now. Many other medications before seemed to lack whatever element it is that Zoloft has that works for me. Occasionally I am prescribed Xanax for my panic attacks. I have not been on Xanax since my mom died. The past year I have been self-medicating on top of whatever doctors have prescribed me. I have been in and out of my Gastroenterologist's office more times than I can remember this past year and 90% of the reason for that is because I was drinking alcohol with my Xanax and my Zoloft on top of the weed I smoked. Poisoning myself to numb the feelings that my mom's death would bring to me. She died and I still do not know if she knew how much I loved her. On her last morning here on Earth after drinking copious amounts of coffee with my Xanax bottle in my purse as I popped the top when I needed to not feel for a while and also hitting my one hitter several times, I walked down the hallway to her hospice room as it was the last room to the left in the building. I sat down beside her, gently sitting my twice microwaved coffee beside her on a nightstand near her bed and playing her favorite band's top hit on my music app on my phone. It's so silly now how the Bay City Rollers "Saturday Night" is so comforting to me. It was the most perfect March morning as I opened the blinds to her Hospice room and we welcomed the sun as the morning frost was melting in slow motion and I sang the songs that remind me of her the most. It was the most beautiful last day. All of her brothers and sisters and parents, her own children and their children, her nieces and nephews. So much light and laughter packed into one room that day she left us. I know that a part of me died in that room but my God it was such a beautiful day.

Proudly, I can say that I have not had an

alcoholic beverage in over a week. I do not remember the last time I went an entire week without drinking. My mom used to bribe me to clean the entire house with wine or vodka along with a pack of cigarettes. Apparently, that is not healthy behavior between child and parent. I had an entire closet full once when I was twenty years old, filled with plastic vodka pints, wine bottles, Four Loko cans, plastic Canadian Mist bottles. Half of that was from my mom bribing me to clean and the other half was acquired through friends and boyfriends that were of age.

I did some really stupid things in order to get a drink. The first time I remember actually blacking out was the summer after I had turned 15. You see, my dad and stepmom let my sister and I have wine coolers here and there as a treat so when my friends brought over a bottle of Smirnoff, I had assumed it was a giant wine cooler. I was obviously a total idiot. I was drinking vodka like water at one point and my friends decided it would be a good idea to make a gravity bong to smoke weed out of two, 2-liter soda bottles, this night would also be the first night that I got high on Marijuana. These "friends," of mine then drove us all to the Waffle House 20 miles away. I am told I passed out at the counter. My friends laughed and joked with the workers telling them I was just really tired. I threw up all over the interior of that dick's car. Oops.

From the car vomit in which I have no memory of, I was then left at my "friend's," uncle's house. I also had no memory of being dropped off at the known pedophile's house, and although I don't remember her leaving me there, I do remember waking up there. I woke up extremely uncomfortable on a bench in an unknown hallway. What I failed to mention is that I was supposed to be babysitting my younger brother the night I first got blitzed. My dad and my stepmom were out of town for the night with their friends and I was supposed to be making sure my 11-year-old brother was safe. Instead, I woke up next to a fat, white, balding, pedophile sitting next to me in his whitey tighties, as I was screaming and asking if my brother was okay. I didn't know exactly what I was drinking until it was far too late. I left my 12-year-old brother that I was supposed to be babysitting to go to the waffle house and pass out. I unknowingly was left at a stranger's house and awoke panicking that these intruders were in my home and I needed to make sure my brother was safe. I was such a failure. My dad obviously found out the next day when he arrived home and I was not there. I was dropped off by a car that I had never sat in and would never sit in again, he was the cousin of my good "friend." My dad saw me drunkenly stumble up our driveway, my vomit from the previous night had formed a glue-like substance, gluing my hair to the side of my face. I had one shoe on and was barefoot on the other foot. My eyes were bloodshot, and the hot July sun was burning my already red retinas as well as my skin. I saw my father standing at the top of the driveway with the biggest look of disappointment in his eyes. It was the day of our community yard sale, and he made me sit outside with him the entire time hungover as my punishment. Punishment for being manipulated and abused but I guess I deserved it. I was such a failure.

> *It's not that I want to die,*
> *It's that I don't want to live,*
> *I take what I am given,*
> *But what is it I give?*
> *I give my time,*
> *I give a smile,*
> *I give a dime or two,*
> *But it's never worth the while.*

After the summer heat burned my stomach into knots of unknowing my future and my skin was burned with cigarettes at parties, I decided that I wouldn't allow others to see my body. I started to wear baggy clothes that would cover my body from the neck down. I made friends with the skateboarders and decided that skateboarding would be my new muse. I don't like to brag, but I am like the worst skateboarder ever. We would skate after school in an empty parking lot across from a church. My grandfather now is renting an old folks home just a few blocks from that empty lot. Unfortunately, I have two biological grandparents left on this planet and my grandfather is losing his fight. He has been suffering from congestive heart failure for a long time now and the amount of cigarettes and alcohol he consumes daily has taken its toll. The friends that I used to skateboard with eventually became like a second family to me. They started a punk rock band after high school ended and I was their groupie. One of the boys even asked me to be his prom date in my tenth-grade year. He has since come out as homosexual which makes me even more upset for the way he treated me in front of the other boys. I was a throw away wannabe groupie to that group of boys. I really thought they liked me and appreciated me but really they didn't see me at all.

After attending a makeshift make out party in Pennsylvania which sounds exactly like what it was, I again thought that maybe one of the boys or girls liked me. My friends and I had been drinking and laughing and kissing all night and when the clock ticked quickly toward the morning hours, we all called it a night. I went upstairs with one of the boys and we took the makeout party well past just that. There are only bits and pieces that still hang in my head of that night and my friends were trying to convince me that a used condom was mine. They scared me into believing that I had lost my virginity to one of those boys that night which I didn't. Years passed and I would go to every one of their band practices and every one of their local concerts. One of the boys who I considered to be a good friend of mine stripped me in a room of our friends and I still feel unclothed. I was wearing a knee length, flowy, aqua colored skirt, and my period briefs as it was time for my period. He pulled my skirt the whole way down to my feet exposing my period briefs to an entire room of boys. Bad people can do good deeds every once in a while, just as good people can do bad. I went years thinking that I had people that loved and cared for me when I had my blindfold covering the facts.

I hung out with these people for half of my high school years, and I thought that they were my friends. Once on a drunken summer night in my teenage years my friend told me I couldn't have any food until I flashed my breasts at one of them. I was hungry before my eating disorder, so I did what I was told. Being bribed and sexually assaulted and abandoned most of my life has taught me one major thing. One of these boys was a crush of mine in my high school years. When I was older, I actually was invited to the same house party as he, several cities away. I wasn't as physically attracted to him as I was when I was a teenager, but I still figured we could hangout and I drove us to the party. He was the first boy I did anything sexual with a few years prior and I was so bad at it that he finished the job himself. I didn't think I would ever see him again or I hoped I wouldn't at least. After many drinks, he wanted me to sit on his lap, he wanted me to do things and I didn't. I eventually hid in my friend's bathroom at the house party until I was sure he was passed out. Her laundry area was in a closet in the bathroom, so I laid on the washer and dryer and cried myself to sleep until early the next morning when I drove away alone leaving him there. YOU HAVE CONTROL. I didn't know it then, but lord do I know it now. Alcohol has robbed me of half of my life and so many relationships and there are so many magical moments I will not get back. My wedding day I had been drinking since the sun came up, up to the point of blacking out at home after our ceremony and reception. I wish that I remembered that whole day but I mainly can layout events in our photo album to compile my own memories. My husband and I hope to have a ten-year vow renewal next fall. I can picture it, it's so beautiful, and I am sober. My drunken Waffle House friends still add me on social media sites as if nothing ever happened. I doubt we will ever talk about the way they assaulted me and took what little dignity and innocence I had. It has taken me a very long time to find confidence again. I still don't really love myself, but I do like myself, or at least I think I am starting to.

Appearance wise I would say I honestly am quite average. Often people think I am much younger than what I really am and now that I am in my thirties, it feels good. My mom took my little brother and I out to eat at Friendly's one afternoon when I was in my early twenties. I ordered a huge meal and an ice cream sundae because ice cream is really easy to coat the stomach to purge. The waitress brought my sundae and apologized as she lost my cherry. I snickered. The waitress said, "oh my sweetie, aren't you a little young to laugh at that?" I replied no that I was 20 and she had asked what my secret was. "Cigarettes and alcohol," was my reply. I still do not know how I am still here. Water, tea, coffee, and the occasional ginger ale when my tum tum does not feel top notch. That's all I drink anymore which I would like to think is why my skin has treated me kindly through the years. This May will be three years since I learned I have a brain deformity called Chiari Malformation type 1. Spina Bifida is a much worse version of what I have but they are in the same Chiari Malformation category. If you have never heard of this, basically our skulls are too small for our big, beautiful brains. That's right, it's 2020 and no brain shame here. Our brains are too big and coincidentally our skulls are too small, therefore a part of our brain called the Cerebellar Tonsils herniates through our skulls, in turn putting pressure on our spinal cords and creating an extensive number of symptoms. But the neurosurgeons I have seen are not impressed by my herniation. That's cool, hashtag me too. After traveling to a very well-known teaching hospital, my mother, and mother-in-law and I found out that I may not be eligible for the decompression surgery because of a connective tissue disorder I was believed to have. Ever heard of an elastic girl? Ehlers-Danlos Syndrome, the hyper mobile type is what my neurosurgeon was spitting out of her mouth. It definitely didn't roll off the tongue. Ehlers-Danlos syndrome is a genetic connective tissue disorder that in my case results in hyper-extensive connective tissue and joints. AKA I'm super bendy.

Stop feeding me lies,
I'm making myself sick,
This used to be my happy place,
Home sweet home darling,
The air is too thick to breathe.

From an early age I remember that I had medical problems that questioned a lot of doctors. Of course, the common procedures I had as a child; tubes in my ears, tonsils and adenoids out, Appendectomy, wisdom teeth. It was summer after fifth grade when I got my first period. My sister thought it was super cool and she welcomed me with open winged pad arms to the womanhood club. She was thrilled, I was devastated. So when my stomach started hurting to the point of holding my breath and grinding my teeth in seventh grade, I had no idea what was happening. This wasn't like my stupid period, this was intense. It was the day following September 11th 2001. Everyone in America was in a hyper state of living as we had just been attacked the previous day by terrorists. I'm sure you've heard of it, most of us will never forget. I walked home from school with my sister that afternoon clenching my stomach but smiling through the pain. I laid in my day bed for hours and hours it seemed until my mom returned home from work. My sister was getting annoyed with me and my pain and hey, so was I. As soon as I saw her car pull up outside our home, I hobbled down the stairs bending over forward at this point, clenching my abdomen in pain. My mom asked me to quickly get in the car and she rushed me to the ER where we waited for what felt like a decade to be seen. That turned out to be the night I had my Appendix out. My mom called my dad to tell him to come if he wanted to visit me in the hospital as I was having an emergency Appendectomy. He was too busy as always though, he had to put his son on the bus for school the following morning....18 hours later.

There were moments throughout the year following my Appendectomy in which my heart would flutter right out of my chest. Later we learned they were called heart palpitations and I was diagnosed with a heart murmur. That became the year the middle school boys started calling me heart murmur. Kids can be so cruel. After a few trips to a local cardiologist I was given a stress test at the ripe old age of twelve. The cardiologist then did this really wild test that I now know is called a tilt table test. He had me lie down on a table that had this wild medieval crank on the right side. Once I was lying down, he strapped me into these leather belts, one around my forehead, one around both hands, and one large one around my ankles, so I was fixed to the table. He then cranked the crank on the side of the table until I was perfectly perpendicular to the floor. This felt so weird, and my limbs went all tingly and eventually numb. As he cranked the crank to lower me back flat, I lost consciousness. I could hear my mom talking to the cardiologist, I could see as my eyes were open, but I was frozen. That was an awful feeling. Spoiler alert, I failed the test and was then diagnosed with POTS aka Postural Orthostatic Tachycardia Syndrome.

My bologna had a first name and it was SVT. Supraventricular Tachycardia is basically a super-fast heart rate. I had to wear heart monitor halters that summer, some that were to be worn only for 24 hours and some that were to be worn for an entire week. It felt like a weird science experiment. My entire eighth grade gym class year was spent on the sidelines drinking Gatorade because my cardiologist didn't want my heart rate to rise too much. Finally, my mom and I had caught an "episode," as we were told to call them on the monitor. My sister and I were home playing in the living room after school one afternoon. My heart felt as if it just took a break and let the hummingbird takeover. I was able to call an ambulance in time for the SVT episode to continue in order for the Paramedics to record it. My pulse was 250 beats per minute at resting. To put in perspective, the average heart rate at a resting state is 75 beats per minute. The Paramedics then injected me with an IV and told me they were going to give me medication in my IV to get my heart beating back to normal. My heart stopped beating. At that moment I felt nothing at all, everything was still and calm. The IV medication worked and my heart began beating at a regular pace. On October 4th, a few short weeks later, we checked into a children's hospital for me to get Cardiac Ablation. It was my thirteenth birthday but just how lucky was I?

At the time I was having my Heart Ablation there were gun snipers in the DC area, picking off people left and right. We were in the heart of DC and the amount of paranoia was justified. My dad did not visit me in the hospital after I had my heart surgery on my birthday. He didn't like driving to the city due to the DC traffic. Driving in the heart of DC during the DC sniper attacks to get her daughter to the hospital for a very much needed heart procedure was probably not something my mother wanted to do either, but hey she did it anyway. She was always there for me no matter what. Her last week here on Earth I made a plan to visit her as much as possible so even if it was just twenty minutes that I could stomach watching my mom fade away I did it. I knew there was going to be a time coming soon that I would not be able to visit her so I was going to be there for her the way she was always there for me. You're supposed to love your mother. You're supposed to take care of them as they age. I loved her so very much, but I did not like her very much for the majority of my life.

I was angry at her for the way she raised us or rather didn't raise us. I was so consumed in my addictions which robbed me of a relationship with her and many of my friends and other family members. I would drive to the nursing home where mom was living for the last few months of her life and take the elevator down to the basement level. At this point her feeding tube was removed and we were waiting for the inevitable. Taking off my winter coat and dropping my belongings on the floor where her urine bag dragged, collecting the little waste her kidneys were able to still get rid of. I would crawl into her bed and lay my head on her sunken chest listening to every slow beat of her heart, every deep and heavy breath. This was my mommy, the one I cuddled when I was sad or scared, she held my secrets, she held my hand. I thought that maybe if I could give off some of my life, she could take some in and be okay somehow. Life doesn't work that way and as I lay my head to her chest in her hospice room after she had passed just a moment before I arrived, I swear I could still feel her breathing, I swear I could feel a faint tap from her chest. I wanted it to be real, this couldn't be real, but it was.

Trying to make peace with someone with

whom you have not felt very peaceful with has been the greatest challenge of my life thus far. So many times, I wished bad things would happen to my mom, so many nights after arguing to the point of screaming I wished death would come to her. What I wouldn't give to have one more belly laugh with her contagious laughter. The last day that I saw her before her accident was at my home. She and my sister had stopped by to drop off some kitchen utensils and luckily both my kiddos were home to visit with her. I had just picked my oldest child up from pre-school and we were cleaning up our lunch mess. My youngest child (at the time) was such a mama's baby. Never really was affectionate with anyone other than me. That afternoon we saw a side of that child that we had not yet seen before. He was openly hugging his Nana and laying his head on her and even though I was annoyed that I had to change his clothes after her visit because he reeked of cigarette smoke, it was a really nice visit. I was only a few weeks into knowing that I was pregnant with our third child. He was a complete surprise to my husband and I as my body just really does not accept birth control. My mom and my sister knew that I was contemplating having an abortion because we were already financially unstable as I just lost my job a month before. My mom was standing in the frame of my front door and the cold, March morning was warm from the sunlight beaming behind her. She told me that the decision would be mine, but that no matter what I had her love and support.

I will always feel that guilt of not letting my mom take my kids overnight to spend the night with Nana. Forgiveness is something that I am working really hard on this year. I will forgive myself for the times I asked her to not smoke before she came, or to please shower before she came over to babysit them. I think that only happened like twice. My anxiety damn near doubled once I had children. Postpartum anxiety is now what it's called, there's actually a name to the face. I would excuse myself from work to call my husband to make sure he knew exactly what to do and exactly when to do it and if it wasn't exactly right, then I would lose my shit. Thanks to modern medicine and a healthy dose of medical cannabis I am much better now. I will learn to forgive myself for the moments I lashed out at my mom when really it was just because I was so hungry for anorexia or she wanted to spend quality time together and I wanted to purge our family dinner. She tried, but she didn't know what to do. My mom had her own demons unaccounted for and I couldn't expect her to save me from mine. There are so many missed family outings and laughter and family photos. I forgive myself for my eating disorder and what it did to my relationship with my mom. I hope she knew how much I loved her.

There were times in my first pregnancy when I would still purge. Nothing as bad as before I was pregnant or even married. I can only count on one hand the times I made myself vomit when I was pregnant with our first child. It was not until after his birth that I stopped purging altogether. In many ways my children saved my life, that is a huge one. I want to be here for all the smiles, and belly laughs. I want to stay youthful and healthy so I can chase my grandkids around and goof off with my husband. My reasons are not your reasons. The things I have done and taken for granted in my body, it truly amazes me that I am still here. I am so thankful that I am. Weighing myself daily does not stop and I can't help but look at the calorie count on packaging. However, when I weigh myself now I weigh in on my support and love, I weigh in on everything I have been through and I have pushed through it all to still be here. I count the calories on the packages of chips that I'm shoving into my face next to my husband on the couch as we are relaxing after the kids go to sleep. I count them and look at him and say how many calories are in a serving, we both laugh and keep watching the show. You only live once right?

I must admittingly state that yes, I am an angry person. I have always been an angry person. I do not know if it was due to my upbringing or too many violent television shows or what, but I remember being angry starting around 6 years old. A Ms. Honey knock off was my school counselor in elementary school. She was supposed to help me be calm and relaxed and let go of all this anger I had. All I remember is playing pick-up stix while my dad tried his pick-up lines. We both struck out. Ms.

Honey was definitely not interested in my goofy ass dad. I do not know if there were any benefits from knock off Honey, but I do have decent memories of her so I guess that counts. I remember games, and rewards for participating. My stepmother used to tell me as a child how angry I was. "You have a black heart," "you're just like your mother." Ugh. It still stings. I had this idea of a mother growing up and she was not a pleasant person at the time, then my father's wife tells me that I am just like this evil force. That shit stays with you. Am I really an angry person or am I just conditioned to believe that I am? I'm still working through that one. Which came first, the anger or the anger shaming? I still am told this by family members. Am I the toxic one, or are they? I will continue to try and navigate these waters the rest of my life.

A burnt orange SUV was driving through our neighborhood as my son's school bus pulled up. Even seeing the big yellow bus, he did not stop. I ran out there with my other children like a goddamn idiot, throwing my arms and my voice around like I had authority. I have no filter. Also something I am still working through. I ran out there and yelled at the man while my blood was boiling and my heart was pounding, he was so wrong. No, I was. The man pulled into our driveway and me, with my 130 lb, 5'5" self-walked over as if I was going to kick this grown man's ass. He was smiling, what a fucking lunatic. He said, "dear, the bus driver didn't pull her stop sign until I was already passing, so I quickly threw on my brakes." Instant blood drain, pooling in the soles of my feet. I felt like a ghost stricken by reality, you're dead! I apologized over and over and shook his hand in order for him to hopefully accept my apology. I am working on this angry black heart, I am going to be better, I won't be just like my mother.

I met my husband in our hometown on his front porch. So darling right? You see, I had a ticket to a concert that I very much wanted to attend but my car situation was vacant, and I had no way to the concert that was well over 3 hours away. My friend at the time suggested that I ride down with her and her friend. I gladly accepted the non-invite invitation. We parked outside of his house across the street in the parking lot. It was a city side street, so parking was pretty limited. Walking over to his house I noticed that my brand-new tights had a huge hole in them. The first thing I said to my husband was, "Can I use your bathroom?" Love at first ripped tights? I changed my tights and the three of us were on our way to Richmond, VA. We stopped at a Wendy's to get something to eat, he was vegan, I was anorexic, there was nothing there for us. When we arrived at the arena where the band was playing, I saw my very recent ex boyfriend in line as well... with his girlfriend. Punch to the gut. I loved him so much, he was my first everything. Getting shitfaced was the only thing I cared about at that point.

Drink after drink after drink after cigarette after cigarette. My friends and I made our way up to the front of the crowd to see the bands. I was good and glowing at this point when I gave my husband my dooey eyes. We kissed. It was sloppy and I was very drunk, but I remember it. The whole way home from the concert felt like a dream to me. Letting go of a love I knew to find a love that was brand new. When we finally got back to our hometown, the city side street, we parted ways with the third wheel. I was still super buzzed and super vulnerable. All I wanted to do was make out and sleep with him, he wanted to know me. This was new. So we went for a walk on that cold march early morning, down the side streets of what I later came to know as our first neighborhood together. Snow started falling and gently laid softly and chillingly on our cheeks. Love at first sight is lust, while lust at first sight becomes love. I moved in a few months later, a month after that he asked me to marry him, two months after that we were married, and four months after that we were expecting our first child. We named him after the lead singer of the band's concert where we first fell in lust.

This past year after my mom's death I really am working toward being a better human. I really am not a good person and I have known that for a while now. I first knew I was a shitty person when I started stealing money. At the time I didn't understand why I was doing it or why I became hungry for theft. Now I know I was feeding my addictions. My addictions to cigarettes, alcohol, and my eating disorders. I have had many jobs over the years, but thankfully only two of them I stole money from. One was a gym and the other was a furniture store. The gym I worked for was well known nationwide, I would never steal money from a mom and pop shop, I'm not that awful. From there I stole from a boy I was seeing at the time, he caught me. I lied to get out of it as I always did. I was a really good liar, my biggest lie was the one where I told myself that I was a good person. These encounters thankfully did not last long and I knew that what I was doing was wrong. It was 2009 then, the year before I tried to kill myself for the second time.

Karma is important to me, therefore if there is a time I can be kind or helpful to someone, I will do it. I will forgive myself for being a shitty human from 16 years old-21 years old. Five years' time is not very long in the grand scheme of things. Looking back now, I see that the entire time I was a shitty human, I was seeing the same boy off and on again. Something that he wanted to do too often was to go on breaks, which at the time I fussed and I cried and I didn't understand. I was so angry. He always told me it was to be by himself, but I now know it was just to fuck another girl. I was physically and mentally abused by this person over the course of five years. Manipulation can truly break a person. Over the course of our relationship breakups and makeups I cannot even count on two hands the amount of women he left me for. Abandoned and desperate, my addictions never left me. They were always there to dry my eyes. I still dream about him but the dreams are never pleasant. They are dreams of jealousy, resentment, anger, sexual tension, and heartbreak. My entire life is built on these dream blocks of those emotions, okay I think I'd like to self-destruct now. A burnt down forest always grows back greener and even more livelier than the previous forest.

My home smells like freshly baked banana bread baked by yours truly. I've loved to create in the kitchen from a young age and I love it even more now. So my specialty as a kid was nothing I would pitch to a fast food restaurant, but it got me by. I would grab a mostly clean bowl from the cabinet, a can of tuna, the tub of mayonnaise in the fridge, and a fork. Half the time I didn't even think I used bread, just whipped up my famous, "cat souffle," as I called it and sat alone in the kitchen eating my tuna mayo out of an already crusty bowl with a fork. My palette has become a little more refined I would like to hope. I have never been very good at baking, only cooking. My husband tells me how easy baking is because you just follow the directions. Woah now buddy, I have never and probably will never follow the directions. Life is supposed to be fun and unpredictable in our own way, following directions seems so bland and boring. Variety is the spice of life right? Make mine spicy please.

Thanksgiving and Christmas were my mother's favorite holidays and she would always make the same dish to bring every year. No one complained though because it was mom's baked macaroni, and it was always incredible. I wish I had asked her for the recipe when she was still alive. I have tried a handful of times to recreate her baked macaroni with the ooey gooey cheese throughout and the crusty noodle edges with the burnt cheese that somehow always tasted just right. Every year we would pile our large, loud, family into our nanny's home for the holidays. I would become annoyed as a teenager because I was given this amazing spread of comfort food to binge on but I had nowhere to purge. I would get agitated if I couldn't purge within a certain time frame because I researched it to know I had a precise amount of hours to puke before I got fat. Every year until the year she died. My grandmother doesn't speak to me anymore, only sends Christmas gifts to my children in the mail. No card, no letter, no, "from Nanny." One of my favorite memories of my Nanny is when my mother, sister, she, and I all went down to Baltimore, MD to stay at a hotel for a girls night. We ate junk food and walked around the Baltimore Inner Harbor after visiting the National Aquarium. It was one of the best girl's nights I have ever had. Thursdays were reserved for the girls when I was growing up. Mom would buy my sister and I our favorite junk food at the grocery store and when our little brother went to bed, we would snuggle and snack and watch CSI. I would give anything for one more girl's night.

Perhaps my sister and I could reconnect on Thursdays and have our own girl's night. Family means something so much more as you get older and you realize family isn't just blood. My best friend is someone that I have known since high school, since we both have families of our own now are able to reconnect as our children play together. It really is an amazing thing if you can hang on to a friend for more than a decade. Nearly everything in my life has come and gone too quickly for me to feel comfortable, but my best friend has been a constant. Of course, we have had our arguments as all humans in relationships do, but we are able to communicate and work through it. From dance parties in her bedroom as teenagers, to waking up and seeing her after my attempted suicide, to eventually meeting her son the day he was born. There were two people that visited me after my hospitalization following my seizure after my second attempt at suicide. My best friend was the first one to come and see me, everything was still very blurry, but I can remember her face. She still looks the exact same, she has excellent genes, I guess. The second person that came to visit me was my ex-boyfriend's mom. I took her flowers two weeks ago because she has not been in the best health as of lately. Coincidentally, my mother passed away on her birthday.

The first time I remember witnessing death I was nine or ten years old. It was summertime and my dad's band was warming up for Sara Evans. When you see a crowd, you either 1.) want to know what is happening, or 2.) walk, no, run, the other direction. I saw a crowd of loud country music goers, ah my people, so I tan over to see what all the commotion was about. My dad was telling us to look away, there were several people saying to get back. I stood behind the crowd and watched as a man went into anaphylaxis shock after being stung by a bee. Everything started to swell, and he couldn't catch a breath. Behind the crowd, I noticed a woman crying to herself with her hands over her mouth. I went over to this woman and gently placed my tiny arm around her waist. With my big, blue, eyes I told her that he was going to be okay, that everything was going to be alright. She hugged me and called me an angel. The paramedics arrived in time to save him, and I later found out that she was actually that man's sister. Our dog Lucy died at the veterinarian's office after being hit by a car. She was so sweet. We only had her for maybe a month before the accident. We never left the back gate open but when we came home it swung wide open. I don't know how she got out that day, but it was awfully heartbreaking. My stepdad took me to work for him to take your kid to work day and when we finally came home from slinging burgers at Burger king, my mom told us the news. I had the coolest day and ate tons of junk food and now my dog is dead. We buried her on my grandparent's property in my blanky that I had since infancy. I loved that blanky and so did Lucy, I thought maybe she would be comfortable in heaven with our favorite blankie. Everyone at my grandparent's house kept telling us not to look outside as she was buried. So of course, I lied and said I needed to use the restroom. I put the toilet seat down and stood on the seat to get a good view out of the bathroom window. Mom slung a half-filled black trash bag into a wet, muddy, hole with all of her weight and proceeded to cover the hole back up with the wet dirt that was pushed aside. Rest in Plastic, Lucy.

After receiving the phone call from my sister regarding my mom's passing I immediately hung up the phone still enroute to her hospice bed and I was screaming where the pit of your stomach connects to the top of your lungs in agony. I don't know what I expected to see. I was mortified to be honest, and I think my memory will not let me forget the fading color of her skin on her ears and her toes or the stillness of her chest. No breathing tube, no IV port, no pulse ox machine, gone as a day from one to the next. No amount of alcohol will make me forget it unfortunately trust me as I have tried. I had just packed a bookbag to go stay with her for the night with my flask and my prescription of Xanax. At this point in her life she was on hospice care, and we knew we were down to her final days. I think I almost expected something amazing to happen, like she would get right out of that hospice bed and start walking and talking again. Every step I took toward her room felt like I had anchors attached to my feet and were weighing me down. I couldn't get there fast enough, but also, what's the point? Her heart no longer held a beat. Her ears were turning blue from the lack of oxygen in her fragile lungs. She was a very heavy smoker for a very long time. Maybe if she stopped smoking her lungs would have been stronger. The maybes and ifs will only consume you if you let them. Don't! Something I have really been trying to follow lately is to live more in the now. Be more present in the present moment. How often do you think you spend worrying about the future? And how often do you spend your day worrying about the past? Live your life and these moments in time will happen naturally. They will come, and they will go, and you will keep moving forward because you have been through a lot of shit. Why not just relax and let life happen with you, not just around you anymore, you have lived that way for far too long.

I always find myself to be the most depressed in the wintertime, absolutely due to the lack of sun and also to the passing of another year. 365 Days used to seem like a lifetime when I was a child, but now a year feels like a month, a month like a week, a week like a day. They don't like to tell you this but having children ages you so much faster than those people who do not have children. As we are grinding the gears in motion to pull us through this winter sludge, I am so excited for what this new year will bring. I have no expectations of anything to come or not to come to us this year, but I do have hope. I hope that this year is better than the last and I hope I can remain sober through this year and the continued years to follow. Hope and expectations are not the same thing but for the past 30 years I have somehow combined the two into a state of panic. My panic attacks happen frequently when I am having PTSD flashbacks. Sometimes I am able to control my moods and I can expect what is to follow an outburst because I have been down that road before. That road is too rocky. I hope that this year I can truly focus on becoming a better human through my medicated mental illnesses. What else do I have to lose other than everything?

I have never been officially diagnosed with obsessive compulsive disorder, OCD, but every day that I write my list of things that need to be done that day, and every time I adjust my shampoo bottles so the brand is facing outward, or the way I fix up the nursery every single day to make it look like a nursery out of a magazine has me questioning if I do in fact have OCD. I have always been this way, as long as I can remember. There really is no reason for me to be a perfectionist. I did not grow up in a home that upheld certain academic standards. My mom never did not care if I got a C or an A, as long as I put my heart into whatever it was that I was working on is all that mattered to me. I grew up with her acceptance and to my understanding, you could love who you wanted, as long as you loved fully. So, I spend the majority of my day making sure that my house is up to my standards. My husband reminds me to pause and to let the kids clean up but the way they clean up is not the way that I would clean up. I have a tendency to panic when adjusting to change, so everything must be just so. How do I break this standard cycle of constantly listing everything that needs to be just so. I forget to breathe, and my body tightens as panic sets in and mania corresponds with the high level of caffeine that I am functioning on.

The first time I can remember physically harming myself was when I was living with my dad and I was in the ninth grade. A movie that I became obsessed with had recently come out on VHS tape, a movie called, "Thirteen." I remember grabbing the kitchen scissors from their compartment in the kitchen and slowly separating the two halves. I dragged a single blade across my left wrist to see what all the hype was about. I can still feel the burning sting that crept slowly across my fair skin. Blood began to seep out immediately and I grabbed a clean washcloth from the bathroom linen closet to wrap around my bleeding wrist. That's what she did in the movie anyway. A lot of my life I would pretend I was in a movie, in my head I would narrate and choose which celebrity would be viewing my life. My life was so dramatic all the time that the only way I could physically deal with living it was to pretend that it was not actually happening and that I was actually playing a role in a movie. The majority of my life was lived this way, this dramatic fantasy world. When I would cut my wrists, my thighs, and eventually my upper arms, I was painting the scene in a movie that no one would ever watch. Thankfully I do not have scars from the many times I cut for the spotlight, I just needed someone to see me.

In the summer following my eleventh-grade year in high school after begging and pleading with my mom to sign me up, I started attending a program for wannabe actors and models. That summer I lost 10 pounds and in return gained a lot of confidence in my appearance and mannerism. When I look back, I can clearly see that there really isn't much of a difference between Barbizon and finishing school. For years I would stand in my older sister's shadow. Both figuratively and literally, as she stood around five feet, nine inches tall and somehow, I ended up at just five feet, five inches. She was the tall, beautiful, blonde haired, and green-eyed sister. I was shorter and wider, and my grandfather even thought I was born with a chromosome disorder as my eyes are so much wider and closer together than hers. I found myself in a comfort zone in the lies and scams in a modeling school for young women. I am so transparent as I am starring in the film of my own life as a background actor. How can I be seen? I needed to be seen. At the same time, I was disappearing, wasting away from starving myself. My mom would take me to the grocery store every Saturday in the summer after eleventh grade and then to the drop off where a bus would take us from our small town to the modeling school outside of Washington DC. At the grocery store she would let me get breakfast and something for lunch that day. I would usually get an energy drink and an apple. I was a cheap date, I guess.

It was very early in the morning when my mom had me weigh myself on her bathroom scale that summer, right in front of her. Fully clothed I weighed in at 95 pounds. She cried because I was so thin and then I cried because I was still so heavy. She and my father found out that summer about my sneaky little addiction to my eating disorder. My dad needed to use the restroom after I had a buffet binge and purge session and decided to drown out the purging noises with the running water from the shower. I had forgotten to flush the toilet and my dad walked in to see my partially digested lunch floating around and sticking to the sides of the toilet as the mucus bubbles floated to the top. He came down to the basement where I went afterwards to rest, and he threw his arms around me as he was crying. Apparently, a former girlfriend of his passed away many years after they dated from an eating disorder. I didn't care, that was not going to happen to me. I was 16 so obviously I knew what was best for me. A few weeks after my dad found out my secret we received print off images of dead anorexics in our mailbox, or as I called it, "thinspiration."

I will give the modeling school some credit for the leaps I took in trying to submerge myself in the actress/model life. With the confidence I gained from attending the modeling school, I went on several auditions for the reality tv show, "America's Next Top Model." Finally, a few years after being shot down for not measuring up to the height requirements, the show was having a special season for short girls. Hello this is my calling! I really am not that short but in the world of high fashion modeling I am. After attending an open call in Washington D.C I was asked to come back the following day for callbacks. This never happened before at the many auditions I went to so this must be good news. I met a wonderful young woman in that callback room, and I still try to keep in touch with her as she has a very busy life now as a spokeswoman and role model. To my delight, I received a phone call a few weeks after the callbacks had taken place and I was invited to be on the show. The casting directors saw something in me, and I would be flown out to Los Angeles, CA. The airfare, food, and room and board were completely covered. They saw something in me, they saw me. Finally, someone is looking at me and I can shine.

It was April and my niece's first birthday party was just around the corner when I had to leave my family to go to LA. I signed contracts stating I wouldn't say where I would be going, and I wouldn't say what I would be doing. I was working at a gym at the time when I had to lie about going to visit a sick aunt in California. I arrived at LAX and was greeted by a shuttle driver with my name on a cardboard slate. There were two other young women in the white shuttle with me and the driver as we headed to the hotel we would be staying and filming at.

Once I arrived at where the show would take place, I learned just how real reality tv really is. I was one of 32 women in the United States that was flown out for that short girl season. We were all given separate hotel rooms with no keys. The show runners held the keys and my success. We ate our meals together in a large conference room but we were not allowed to speak to one another unless there were cameras recording.

My confidence, my hopes, my dreams, my expectations, my arrogance, all of it nosedived and I'm still recovering from the crash. Out of all of the 32 women that were flown out to LA, I was one of the first five to be eliminated. Was it because I accidentally locked myself out of my hotel room, I was having an unmedicated panic attack and I tried to let myself back into my room, but I failed. Was it because they went through my suitcase when we were filming, and they found my stash? I was abusing laxatives at this time in my life and my suitcase was lined with cigarettes, nighttime cough syrup, and ex-lax. When I was eliminated very early on in the show, I lost every bit of self-esteem I worked so hard on building the past three years. From LAX to Dulles, I was booked for a red eye back to my cardboard town. My badass paternal grandmother died six weeks after I got back, I lost my job two months after that, and two weeks after losing my job, my boyfriend with whom I just moved in with a few weeks prior had broken up with me. Five months later his mom would visit me after I attempted suicide for the second time. Hospital beds would become my home sweet home because I felt safe and taken care of.

All I wanted was your city bed,
Your shaking hands,
And your fucked up head,
I could have had the world,
But I just wanted your hometown,
My name could have been in lights,
But you wouldn't be around,
I plant my feet and grow,
Grow on up buttercup,
Your love is putting on a show,
I despise these old episodes.

I returned home from LAX and unfulfilled dreams to drive straight to a hair salon with my mother. The show runners for ANTM booked me a red eye flight back home and after binging on the shitty pizza the showrunners bought the leftover women, I was wide awake in a zombie pizza state. My mom knew how heartbroken I was, and she really tried to offer me anything she possibly could to make me feel better. She thought I sabotaged myself to get off the show because my boyfriend at the time thought it was so stupid to model. He made jokes about my appearance and the modeling world and how dumb they both were. I loved him so much. Truly, I never was told why I was eliminated, just that I wasn't good enough. Like always.

My mom picked me up at Dulles and we drove to a very crappy hair salon, in her very crappy car, in my hometown and I told them to cut it all off. I don't know what I was expecting when I told the hairstylist to give me a super short pixie cut, but

I left with a super short pixie cut. Looking at my stupid head in the fold out vanity mirror attached to the passenger visor in my mom's car, I saw a very tired, pale, ugly, loser, freckled, boy. I hated everything about myself at that point. Two months after that my grandmother sat outside in the shade of a tree under three blankets in late May. She was freezing cold and just two weeks after that she passed away. She frequented the hospital with her many illnesses related to her lupus, but this time was different. This time she was airlifted to Hershey Medical Center. This time I didn't get to say goodbye like I always have before.

> *My bed still holds your bones,*
> *In my closet, hangs your clothes,*
> *My black heart holds your memories,*
> *I lack your hand to hold.*

My employer at the time would not let me leave my job in order to go visit my dying grandmother before someone else would come in and relieve me of my receptionist duties. I pulled up to the hospital in time to see the helicopter lift off into the warm June sky and that's the last chance I got to be that close to her living body. Two months after my grandmother's death I moved in with my boyfriend at the time, his friend, and his friend's girlfriend. We'll call his friend Jim and his girlfriend

Satan. My boyfriend had cheated on me many months before with Satan on top of the countless other women and Satan called me at my work and gave me detail by detail of every item of clothing that came off and in what order. So, I moved in with Satan and Jim and stranger boy because I loved that stranger boy and I wanted to do whatever he wanted me to do to make him happy and love me because he meant so much to me. Satan pulled her puppet strings while bringing up past flings during one of mine and stranger boy's many "breaks." Stranger boy was allowed to fuck which ever other women he would deem doable on our breaks and do as he pleased, but I was to remain close and tight on the leash he had hand made for me. When a stranger boy found out that I too had a fling on a break he broke up with me and I was to leave the apartment I had moved into with them. I packed my essentials with tears streaming down my face and realized how much of a failure I was right then and there.

I failed at being on a television show, I failed to hold down a job, I failed to hold down my food, I failed at saying goodbye to my dying grandmother, I was such a fucking failure I thought. I drove to my mother's home that I had left just a month prior and told her I was going to kill myself if I didn't get help. That was the night that I willingly checked myself into a mental hospital a half hour away from my home because I knew I couldn't be left alone, not now.

Once arriving at the mental hospital by

ambulance I was then told to undress in a room alone and empty my pockets as well as my purse. I stood in a paper towel-esque gown as I was asked to stand on a scale, against a yard stick on the pale-yellow wall, and probed on why I needed to be there. The nurse at the reception and check in area gave me the rundown on how things worked around the facility and after turning myself into their hands for my mental health care, the minimum amount of days that I would stay for evaluation was four days there was no maximum. It was August and the sun was so blazing hot as it would bounce off of the black gate that contained us nuts like a fence that you couldn't see any light through surrounding the smokers cove.

Every hour on the hour we had smoke breaks and every hour on the hours I would hurt my lungs a little just to get some smokey, august, air. Sometimes I would smoke and sometimes I would just sit out there staring at the black fence wondering if I would ever be able to fix my little black heart. I was one of the lucky ones at the mental hospital and I didn't have to share a room with anyone. It was just me, a nightgown, a shitty excuse for a blanket, and I think a bag of flour for a pillow. We were able to make phone calls outbound at certain times of the day, but we were not allowed to receive incoming calls. I called my boyfriend and confessed my love and apologized and told him that I would be better for him. He promised to see me when I got out and we would work on things. That never happened. Empty promises were my backbone seemingly. At the mental hospital we participated in art therapy as well as one on one therapy to see what sort of program we would need based on our own individuality. I was diagnosed bipolar and after sitting down for an exit interview with my mom and the psychiatrist I told them I was better and after willingly checking myself in four days prior, I packed my bags and checked myself out.

When the tide rose high,
You cursed the sky,
The silence thrashed and fell,
And you cursed yourself,
But they all wished you well,
Then the sun rejoined the clouds,
And you cursed the one in charge,
He promised eternity, he promised you life,
So you spat at his faith, you hated his wife,
You've never been able to go out on your own,
Knowing you at all, they shouldn't leave you alone,
You'll scratch and pick until it makes you sick,

This time you've cursed your claws,
With every creature seen in your dreams,
Their eyes so bright, the words they beam,
Once the day comes, you lay your demons to rest,
That's when he loved you most and saw you at best.

My husband and I have been living in our current home for almost four years now. My dad likes to tell stories of when all four of us lived together in a farmhouse. I don't remember my parents ever being together as they were divorced before I was even two years old. The first home I remember as a child was a poorly built brick apartment complex. We were on the second floor which I thought was super clever of my mom because floods can happen anywhere. I guess I was already paranoid at three years old, but I had good reason to be. The first time I remember seeing a gun was when the barrel was pointed right in my direction. I was probably four or five years old playing outside in the leaves with my sister. It was autumn so my birthday had either already passed or was very soon to come. A man shouting across the apartment building corridor was holding something in his white, chubby, hands. His voice is echoing in my chest now, "run little girl or imma shoot you." I froze. No stupid child, get up and run, run faster than your legs can take you. It wasn't really a run as much as it was a sprint that day. I am now invisible. I slithered like a snake up the stairs to the second floor and into 1022F. If he can't see me then he won't be able to shoot me. With my pounding heart I tearfully told my mom about the incident, and she immediately called the police and they arrived in a timely manner to investigate. She was always there for me when I needed her the most. I only wish she was there for herself more. If only she knew how much I loved her.

When my mom remarried it was at a courthouse and my baby brother was already two years old. Their relationship was always so strange to me. They would yell and fight and throw things and then twenty minutes later they would be sitting on the couch laughing and smoking. I cannot recall the exact reason we went to the shelter, it may have been the time her husband chucked a huge ashtray at her, but when my baby brother was an infant my mother checked herself and her three children into a shelter for women of abusive relationships. We walked up a few flights of old wooden steps and we were shown a room that was to sleep all four of us. There was a wooden cradle where my mother laid my brother down to sleep and my mom, sister, and me would all share the full-sized bed. The room was dark and dusty. The walls were peeling wallpaper slightly in the corners where you could see a tacky yellow slime seeping through. There were no curtains in the room either so the city streetlamps were creating an orange glow that made every eerie shadow seem even darker. I think I probably slept there for an hour. Awoken by the sounds of women laughing and babies crying, I walked myself down to the communal kitchen and mess hall that were on the first floor of the building. I sat down and re-wrapped the blanket around my shoulders because it fell off while I was walking, and the old building was very drafty in the winter time. A woman walked out from the kitchen and asked if I would like a bowl of cereal. I shook my head yes and she faded away only to return with a knock off brand of cheerios in a bowl of milk and a spoon. We stayed at that shelter for less than 24 hours but somehow it felt like we had been there for weeks.

I have recently started telling my family about my alcoholism and so far the biggest response I have gotten is, "I know." There are so many times that I still feel abandoned and most of it is because of the relationship my sister and I have with our mother. It's the ski trip we never took as kids, it's all the broken promises that have built who I am today. Lying was my scapegoat and I ended up getting really good at it. The boy I dated from the age of 16 to the age of 21 slowly became my lying punching bag so to speak. There are many times that he was in the wrong for the way he treated me and left me for other women only to return and make me feel like I was the one he loved. My intimacy, love, jealousy, and trust grew from a place of wrecked plans and broken hearts. I have only been with two individuals as a sober person. Anyone in between was a background actor in my love life film. One was my first boyfriend, and one is my husband. Alcohol was the fire, lying was the fuel, I had everything that I needed to self-destruct and I was really good at it. I forgive myself for being a shitty partner. Anytime my husband and I argue I usually overreact because I am dramatic, or so I'm told. I tell my husband that he deserves better than me, that I am worthless, that I am not a nice person, and that I am a lying bitch with a black heart. "You are just like your mother." I will never be that tall blonde who is always smiling and making the world a better place. I'm just trying to exist at this point.

Robots in three by fours,
Checking our wrists,
Watching the doors,
Forgetting what we came here for in the first place.

My mom was a very strong woman and she knew it. Her biological father passed away before she was born from a heart condition. Her own mother taught her to be strong and independent I suppose. My mom was the oldest of three children all through different fathers. My aunt's father was the one who stayed through everything and is still with my nanny today. My mom also did not have the best childhood as she would tell me horror stories of her parents and the way they treated her. The apple doesn't fall far from the mentally ill apple tree. She would tell me how they would embarrass her and shame her for some issues my mom had with her bladder that would result in bedwetting as a child and a pre-teen. I could not believe how brave my mom was to still be here to tell me these stories. My dad has told me a few stories himself of living with my mom and the way she treated my dad. She was so far gone in her own addictions that her relationships were dwindling and she self-medicated to make her brain stop hurting. Mental illnesses can be so unfair to every life it taunts. The only memories I have of my parents ever being together are of when they had to forcefully come together for a school event or birthday party and even then, the tension took over the room with its thick haze.

My dad would visit me in school sometimes and he would come have lunch with me and make all the kids at the table laugh. For those 30 minutes on these afternoons, I was cool because my dad was cool. Most of my lunch period in middle school was spent eating my school food in the bathroom. There was a group made up of three girls that made my middle school years twice as hard as they should have been. They would call me names and make fun of my appearance and the clothes I wore because I was much poorer than they were. I grew up ashamed of who I was, so I tried to stay hidden. I would walk through the cafeteria with my head hung low and slip into the bathroom with my orange school lunch tray. I would lock the door of the stall behind me and for those 30 minutes I was alone, and I was safe. No one ever really enjoys middle school, it's a transitional period in all of our lives. These bitches made my transition into womanhood feel shameful and scary when it didn't need to be. Every day I would have that burning hot feeling in your veins right where your heart meets your lungs.

In between your chest, it's sharp and it stings. It hurts and at the same time feels almost comforting and routine. The stinging feeling of rejection and a broken heart and loneliness that you can only feel, you can't even come close to describing it. Eventually these girls were the reason I went to live with my dad after eighth grade, the summer right before high school. I called my bullies the KKK in my head as all of their names began with the letter K. The bullying was so bad that I couldn't stand to be around me anymore.

The KKK would tease me about my appearance, my clothing, my home life, my brother being half black and half white, my food, my grades. Everything that I was and I knew was ridiculed and manipulated at home and at school and I hated myself for being so bad. I was bad at school, bad at the girl scouts, bad at being pretty, bad at making friends, bad at lying. My stupid bad black heart. I started writing poetry when I was six years old and eventually, I would turn them into little songs that my sister, my brother, and I would later perform as a band in front of our dad and my step mom. Writing gave me an outlet to express how I felt without having to tell anyone and I wasn't bad at it. I wrote my first children's book when I was in the eighth grade and later my mom and sister had it printed for my first son. I started to fill notebook after notebook with my emotions and doodles throughout each day. Even if my home life wasn't a dream come true and even if my school life was full of fear and abuse, I had my notebooks.

Every single cycle, one week before my "time of the month," I become a monster. I know it is most likely hormones but during that time, I don't want to be around myself when I am premenstrual. Every month I secretly hope that we get pregnant again but this time with a daughter. I know that our chances are slim and even more slim the older I get. We are so lucky to have three biologically beautiful boys, but I will always grieve for the daughter I will never have. As they grow as individuals, we will encourage them to pursue the life that they feel best suits them, but for now they identify as boys. I think ever since my first niece was born was when I decided I want to have a daughter. Everything was dainty and pretty with a fragility only a daughter could supply. With the relationship my mother and I had I could only dream of what it would be like to have my own daughter someday and how I would treat her well, like a princess. We are beyond blessed to have the three children we have today, and I would not change a thing about who they are. This doesn't mean I cannot long to have that mother daughter bond someday, but I know that my husband doesn't want any more children. I get it, it is a lot of work raising three humans and keeping yourself alive. My heart holds so much love these days and all of these sleepless nights and shitty diapers will someday be just a memory. I'm so afraid that my heart just isn't ready for the foggy baby haze phase to end.

We conceived our first born due to a lack of education on my doctor's part when they prescribed me anti depression medications on top of my birth control pills. I was on the fertile combo for just over three months before we found out that we were expecting. I was in shock after a cheap dollar pregnancy test showed a second line very faintly and I frantically asked my husband to go get a better-known brand because surely this one was wrong. I was only one or two days past my normal cycle start date, but my breasts felt heavy and sore. My husband and I were babysitting my oldest niece and as he set the tv up for the two of them to watch "A Very Goofy Movie," My heart dropped as I saw two pink lines quickly appear and stay. We were pregnant. I was terrified. What was my body going to go through? How fat was I going to get? I hope it's a girl I thought. My husband was so excited and assured me that we were going to have so much fun.

I had a smooth first pregnancy and our first son was born after 16 hours of labor and only 15 minutes of pushing. My midwife later called me a birthing machine, I'll take that title proudly. I had hoped to have a water birth with my first child but unfortunately there were no birthing facilities nearby that had a birthing pool and my family had talked me out of the idea. I will grieve the water birth I will never experience but I forgive myself for dreaming of that moment. Our second child was conceived as we both decided when our oldest son was two that we would try for a sibling. It took six months of trying before seeing a fertility doctor. I had a blocked fallopian tube and after that was unblocked, it only took two weeks before I saw those two, pretty, pink, lines show up. My second pregnancy was again uneventful until around sixteen weeks when I had become itchy all over my body. My husband and I had a private scan to find out the gender of our second child. Please be the girl I had hoped for. Only two minutes into the sonogram and I knew before the tech that we were having a brother! I bawled. The whole way home from the sonogram I cried tears of grief over a daughter I wouldn't have. It was mid-October but the drive home was so rainy I couldn't see through my teary eyes even if I tried. I was ashamed of feeling this way, this is a beautifully healthy child, and I am hot and empty. I will try to forgive myself for having gender disappointment feelings as my feelings are valid and they do matter. The itching all over my body had taken over my entire being at that point. I spent nights crying myself to sleep because my skin burned, and no amount of scratching could make the burn go away. After my twenty-week appointment, the OBGYN addressed my concern with my itching and simply told me that, "you're pregnant you are going to be itchy and uncomfortable." But this was different I thought, I'm in pain and you aren't even trying to help me figure out why I want to rip my skin off. Okay then, time for a new doc.

Between the time of my previous visit to my OBGYN office and the following visit I did some research on itching during pregnancy. What I found made my skin crawl and burn as I was sure that I had this liver condition called, "cholestasis." I discussed having the appropriate bloodwork at my following appointment with the nurse over the phone. Later that afternoon I got the call from my midwife, and I was unfortunately right. I had a liver condition affecting my pregnancy that now made my normal pregnancy a high-risk pregnancy. My own bile acids would be transferred between my gallbladder and liver and in for some dumb reason would back up in my liver, with no place to go, so the bile acids would spill into my bloodstream that I was sharing with my unborn child. My body keeps failing me and now it's failing my children too. After reading about cholestasis and becoming quite informed on the subject, everything in my pregnancy changed. I would have tests every two weeks to make sure my baby was still alive and kicking because having a stillborn baby was something that actually happened with an unmedicated and unmonitored pregnant woman that has cholestasis. I was on a daily dose of a bile acid reduction medication that cost nearly $600 out of pocket every two weeks, anything for my baby. Every two weeks the sonogram technician made sure that my baby was kicking, practicing breathing, and growing on track with the pregnancy. Our second son was to arrive no later than 37 weeks gestation as the odds of stillbirth increased after 37 weeks. Not like I didn't already have trouble sleeping from the cholestasis itches but now I was in fear that my baby could die at any time because of my dumb body. My husband and I set our date to go to the hospital and begin the painfully slow process of induction and welcoming our beautiful blue eyes babe into the world. He came so quickly that our photographer had unfortunately missed his first several moments of life on the Earth. As my mother was such a heavy smoker, I requested she not enter the labor room unless she wore a gown. That all went out the window when I held my second baby. I was just so thankful that he was here, and he was breathing and he was everything that my heart wanted, nothing else in the world mattered. When my first son was born, my mom was awake the whole night in the waiting room periodically checking on me although I knew how pushy she could be. I was trying to keep her distanced during my labor because I did not want any anger or yelling, not that day. When my second son was born, my husband phoned my mom to let her know that her third grandson had arrived. She was quick to get in the car to come see him, too quick to not reek of smoke.

When my husband and I found out that we had accidentally been expecting our third baby in February 2018, we felt gray. I spent the first half of March in bed in tears and in the toilet from vomiting. I held my stomach and bawled knowing I wouldn't be able to keep this child because we were not in a financially well-off place. Gutted, I called several women's clinics, defeated, thinking that was my last resort. I cried myself to sleep nearly every night clenching my stomach with one hand and holding another hand over my nose and mouth. Maybe if I suffocated myself, maybe then I wouldn't have to get an abortion. My mom knew that I was tethering back and forth on the fence between keeping this baby or not and on the day of her accident she made such valid points on keeping it that I rolled my eyes and told her I would call her back later in the day. I didn't. My scheduled "procedure," was early the next morning in Baltimore and I just didn't want to talk about it anymore. I never went to that appointment because later on that night I got the call from my sister that our mom had fallen and was enroute to the hospital. Thank God I could have this baby, thank God I could be a mom for this one too. I held my abdomen with two hands and softly cried myself to sleep, we were safe together. I was very sick in the beginning of my pregnancy, between my mom's accident and the pregnancy hormones I had lost ten pounds and was sick to my stomach a lot. The hospital that my mom was kept at for nearly a month was over two hours away from us and on every trip we made through the rocky overpass I would get carsick. The large, spinning, white, windmills that stood atop of the furthest mountain seemed to drown out any noise that came from inside the car and all I could hear was the whooshing of the wind and the sloshing of my empty stomach. I was so sick, this had to be my daughter. After having cholestasis in my prior pregnancy my chances of having the illness again were very high. At 17 weeks gestation I was unfortunately diagnosed with the liver condition again and was seeing a high-risk specialist. We had a scan at 17 weeks to make sure the baby was still doing well regardless of the liver condition. Rather quickly we saw we would be expecting our third boy in 10 weeks. I wasn't as gutted this time. I needed a name though, I had zero boy names picked out as I was sure that I would have a daughter. Throughout the entire pregnancy I felt robbed. I was robbed of having a daughter, of having a water birth, of having a healthy full 40 weeks of pregnancy, of having my mom there for the birth, robbed of feeling anything in my pregnancy other than depression. Our third son arrived four weeks early as he stopped growing in my uterus, but my God is he beautiful. I went to the hospital to check in and my sister called me. My mom was in the ER just a few floors below us with another one of her high fevers. The day our third baby was born the midwife examined my placenta and told me that it was calcified way beyond where it should have been in the gestational timeline. I quickly got dressed and asked if I could walk upstairs to see my mother in ICU as she had been admitted as I had given birth. Through every birth of my children, she has always been there, she has always been by my side. My uterus ached, my head was light, and I was so, so, hungry. But despite just giving birth, I dressed myself in the hazmat suit that was required when visiting her, I slapped the gloves on my hands and tied the surgical grade mask around my pale, iron deprived face. I greeted my mom with a smile and photos of her fourth grandson, my third boy! She had no idea who I was. Her skin was so hot that the nurses lined her body with ice packs. Her eyes started to get a thick yellow fog to them, blinding her it seemed. She seemed to always have a white tongue anymore from bacteria growing too fast. I don't know why I expected her to sit up with a big smile and tell me how beautiful our third baby was. It hurt, everything hurt, and my mom always made the hurt better but she can't help me anymore. This is a pain I had to accept and let it course through my veins. That's the day I knew we wouldn't have our mom back.

The pain of birth is in no comparison to that of a kidney stone. Not that one is more painful than the other, but they are two very different kinds of pains. In the summer of 2009 following my grandmother's death I started to have this intense back pain that I had never felt before. Running to the restroom thinking that I had to vomit, instead I just had to pee, but my pee was not actually pee but was in fact just red blood. I immediately panicked and the first person I told was my boyfriend at the time, I called him because I was freaking the fuck out. He was busy hanging around town with his friend that day, but he still came to get me from work to take me to the emergency room. I just wish that he would have stayed with me instead of dropping me off in front of the electronic doors of the emergency room. He never stayed. I was so scared and alone and pissing blood. He and his friend drove a few towns away to meet up with some other girl. It was always some other girl, I was never the one. The nurse in the emergency room kindly asked me what my pain level was. I jokingly and painfully asked if she meant the pain in my kidney or the pain in my heart. She told me that the pain medication would help with both and I was so thankful for morphine that day.

Although I have daily pain today mostly related to my chronic Lyme disease, I do not feel the need to be on intense pain medication. Thankfully

I live in a medical cannabis state and am able to take care of my aches and muscle spasms naturally. In the years leading up to my mom's death she was constantly on some pill concoction for her daily pain. After she had her accident where she fell down the stairs at her work, she was in pain daily, mostly in her shoulder and her back. For years she would see specialists and other medical professionals in order to have pain relief. I will never know how much of that pain was in her heart or if she was really in chronic physical pain. My mom had a very addictive personality and any substance she came into contact with she would indulge. Cigarettes, beer, junk food, pain medication, and weight loss programs. I often wonder if maybe she would have taken care of herself better, just maybe she would still be here. Constantly tangled in the maybes and what ifs has anchored me to alcohol through the majority of this past year and I am finally resurfacing. That first breath was a hard one to choke down but steadily I am navigating.

Hospital waiting rooms have felt like home to me ever since I was a child. My mom was a bit of a hypochondriac as far as I can remember as a child so the emergency room staff seemed to know when we would be coming in to see them. Many people fear going to the doctor or perhaps having to be in a hospital makes their skin crawl. For me, I feel comforted by the sterile sheets and steadily beeping monitors. Whenever my mom was sent to the hospital during the year following her accident, I tried my best to be there for her. She unfortunately had many infections back-to-back after her spinal cord injury. I wanted to be able to hold her hand the way she held me and let her know that she was okay and each time I went to see her in the ICU it felt like going home for me. Her rhythmic ventilator slowly hissing oxygen added the white noise that I needed to fall asleep. Through seeing the nurse, the physician, the infectious disease doctor that I personally knew as I saw him a few years before for Lyme disease, and lastly the respiratory therapist. The pitter-patter of white lab coats and clipboards was a slow hum that felt as if the hospital had it's on breath and I was accustomed to this rhythm. She always held me when I needed her the most and during one of our many visits with her at the hospital, she started sobbing knowing she would never hold me again. She asked me if when she left the hospital I would come and spend the night with her and cuddle again like we used to. She was the big, warm, strong human that wrapped me up so tight to kiss my cheek and call me her cuddle monster. I'd tear all the beeps and blips from her wrists in order to carry her home. These were the sounds of the emergency room breathing as if it were inhaling patients and exhaling the steady beeps of mom's monitors, until the day she was unhooked.

We gathered outside of her hospice room into a smaller, "family room." Those who wanted to say their goodbyes would be able to do so shortly.

She arrived at the hospice facility by ambulance from her nursing home. After they alerted us that she had arrived we were then told that per hospice regulations my mom would only be on her ventilator for 30 minutes. We were told to not have much hope and to understand that most patients on a ventilator do not survive long without it. My mom had her immediate family in her room when the pastor said that prayer that will forever make me cry. The valley of the shadow of death had lingered over her crippled body for almost an entire year at this point. For three days my family members and I would come and go to visit my mother. We would laugh and eat and sing and dance in my mom's hospice room.

I haven't spoken to anyone in my mom's family in over six months now. The day my mom died she took a little piece of all of us with her and we just haven't even tried to put the puzzle back together. Communication is the most important thing we can do in this living realm, yet no one wants to try to communicate with one another until it's too late. Maybes and what ifs then start to creep in and self-pity and depression pull you out in the undertow. Instead of giving up and letting the tide take you over, scream. We have to communicate as long as we still have a voice as we have this one chance to be heard so scream if you have to.

Twice this week I have rearranged our pantry as well as our medicine cabinet. I vacuum our rug twice a day in addition to vacuuming the rest of the house daily. I emptied all of the trash cans and recycling bins into their larger counterparts outside which we have to do daily. There were times as children that my sister and I would play a game called hide the ostrich. We would sit in the dirty laundry pile and through our mother's predisposed lingerie at each other. Super gross, but we thought that her dirty silk ostrich was so silly. We always found a way to make our living situation the best that we could. We had our games and sleepless nights where we would count all of the tiles on the ceiling and all of our classmates until we fell asleep. We would fall asleep mid conversation and carry on with our separate lives only to return to this routine we built. It was my absolute favorite time of day.

I looked up to my sister so much and I had hoped that we were secretly twins, I was just shorter and more round than she was. There were times in our middle school years that people would call my sister and I the, "double mint twins." We shared a bedroom for most of our lives as children, so I always had my sister time. There is something really special about raising your own children and seeing the bond between my children breaks my heart most days. I know that one day they won't talk and one day they will feel abandoned by their brother and one day they will question if their brother really does love them or not.

My sister was with me the day that we were jumped in an alley just behind the street our home was on. I was in middle school dating a boy that I had found out was interested in another girl, so I ended things. After we broke off our crush, he and his cousin decided to follow my sister and I home from school. I was ten years old, and my sister was twelve. She was just about to leave middle school for high school and it was our last year walking home together. Chad pushed me in the alley that felt so safe so close to home. His cousin grabbed my sister's arms and held them behind her as if he were an officer and she was under arrest. I turned around to see that Chad was running full speed at me with his head down. I felt a quick sharp pain in my stomach that was shortly followed by my head smacking the asphalt. I thought I heard my skull crack open, but maybe it was just the asphalt splitting. He headbutted me so hard in my stomach that my ears were ringing. No one came to help us. My sister was screaming for help, but no one came. She put out her hand to help me stand up as the boys ran away. She grabbed my hand and helped me up and then we both walked home holding each other, with tears running down our cheeks.

  After middle school my sister went to live with my dad so when I was her age two years later, I followed my big sister's footsteps. It was always as if she had one foot in the door at our dad's house and one foot in the door at our mom's house. I felt like she never wanted to be with me so when I went to live with our dad, she moved back to our mom's. Why was she avoiding and escaping me? She was the one that chased me around the house with knives. What did I do wrong? I lived with my dad for just over two years before my mother and I schemed for me to go back to living with her. My dad's house always felt very open and carefree so why would I want to go back and live with my evil, strict, mother? I really don't know what it was, maybe all the time my friends manipulated and sexually harassed me and I couldn't take it anymore. Regardless of why it happened, it happened, and my mother and I went behind my dad's back one day while I was at school.

My mom let me live with my dad for those two years under one condition, my dad would still have to pay her monthly child support for me. My dad loved me so much that no amount of money mattered to him. There was a student aid who came to get me from my eleventh-grade history class. I knew that meant that our plan had worked, and I was packing up my bags to never see these people again. When I didn't come home from school that day my dad found that note that I left for him. I left a note for my dad on the kitchen table saying that I wasn't coming back and my mom and I drove off to her home in my stupid sad hometown with our stupid little black hearts beating in sync.

Maybe it was because I fell in love for the first time a week before I made the move to my mother. My girlfriends and I found ourselves bored at an all-night diner after sipping sodas and eating cold french fries. It was October 15th and Halloween was just around the corner so we figured what better way to ring in the holiday than to go to a haunted house of all places. My best friend at the time sat beside me at the haunted house until this really cute boy squeezed between us. I didn't know him but my friend ended up making out with the guy and then he looked at me so I thought I was supposed to do the same thing. Is this what people do at haunted houses, I didn't know. The only other time I had been to a haunted house was with my mother when I was six years old. I begged my mom to take me so many times and she finally caved. I panicked after the first skit and as the prisoners of the haunted house walked the maze walls to the basement. My mother liked to always tell people this story because I asked the grim reaper where the exit was. How existential of me.

That was the night a boy that worked at the haunted house mistaken me for my friend and instead of capturing her and taking her through the trapdoor to find a gargoyle that she knew, the now famous drummer captured me, and I went down the trapdoor in his arms and away from the stranger boy I was kissing. I waited in that basement for my friends and a stranger boy and quickly they found me, and we made our way through the dark and spooky haunted house.

Lethargic and nostalgic,
They go hand in hand,
One silver, One gold,
With no one cashing in,
Time is money honey,
This five dollar bill won't get me far,
Drive to work,
Back home, back to work, But sleeping in my car,
Bring a pillow and a blanket, Something to stay warm,
I will bring the laughter,
And comfort from the storm,
All I ever wanted was short story time,
Instead you flashed me those bedroom eyes,
Sure, I said, okay. Not what I meant to say,
I meant to grab my shoes,
And hit the road, but I had left them in the backseat,
The way you think of me.

We then exchanged phone numbers and social media account information and when I looked up his relationship status, his statement was taken. I thought how foolish this stranger boy is to think that we were dating after the haunted house night. Later I learned that he had a long-distance relationship with a girl from the beach. I should have known from that moment that a stranger boy would only break my heart time and time over again for roughly six years, off and on, after breaks and makeouts. He was in his first year of college when I met him and I was in my junior year of high school. I am thankful for all of the friendships and relationships that stemmed from a stranger boy and I forgive myself for staying for so long. I cried myself to sleep for the entire first week of living back at my mom's house.

My bed was a mattress in the corner on the first floor of her townhouse. Instead of a closet, I had my clothing and belongings piled in the water heater closet, along with my mom's cat's litter box. Most days I would go to high school with my clothes reeking of cat piss, was this really better than living with my dad? The majority of my life was spent pleasing others, being manipulated and abused and staying by choice. I forgive myself for thinking that was all that I am worth, I am worth so much more and so are you.

I started attending a new high school on special permission as the school my mother wanted me to attend was not in her district almost immediately after running away to live at my mom's home. Luckily, I met a friend a few months prior that also attended the school so I felt like I already had one foot in even though most of the students I knew from years ago in middle school. WIthout skipping a beat the heart of the high school knew that I was still a garbage human being thanks to the kkk. The whole reason that I went to live with my dad in the first place was because of the bullying these kids put my through and here I was willingly going through it again just to get my heart broken again and again by stranger boy, My friend at the time shared spit with stranger boy as well as her acquaintances. We had some of the same classes, we knew the same people, we shared the haunted house romance, and we were even mistaken for each other a few times. I loved her and I wanted to be just like her.

I was thrown against a locker by my throat once for the stupid mistake of someone mistaking me for her. My friend stole a winter coat out of some popular girl's locker. Automatically it was my fault, and I was thrown with such force and there was no adult in sight. I did everything with my friend during that junior year of high school. From dying and cutting my hair to tripping on cough medicine with her and her friends in a parked car in the school's parking lot. All I wanted was for someone to love me and want to be around me and sometimes for a moment, I thought maybe she was one of those people.

Love is a strange thing. My mother loved me so very much and so very fiercely, but she had no idea how to love someone. My father was able to love me every other weekend until I grew up and decided my boyfriends were far more important than my family. Stranger boy loved me, I think, but he also didn't know how to love. I've been so loved throughout my life by such strange people in such strange ways which is why I love so strangely. I have never openly come out as bi-sexual but I have known since I was ten years old that I am.

It's a needle on a record,
It's a hand on a clock,
Weighing me down, down, down,
Ticking to the tick tock,
Right hand, left hand,
Hand in hand,
Don't hand me off,
Time sits and brews,
As the morning and afternoons pass,
I wasted so much time with you,
Beauty queen with sash and wave,
The attention that you crave,
Although you're forever in denial,
You simply love to hate yourself,
I've never met eyes so empty,
Until I fell in a Haunted House.

I fucked up and I started drinking again, so I failed at being sober. Eighteen days was the longest I have gone without drinking in years. I am embarrassed and discouraged. Maybe I was never really an alcoholic to begin with or at least not anymore. I don't wake up first thing in the morning and require a drink to jumpstart my day. Breakfast isn't set every morning with mimosas, mostly just the same mug of coffee reheated in the microwave many times throughout the day. Nap times are usually spent chasing my toddlers around to get them to sleep and now chased with day old coke sitting out from the night before. When my oldest gets home from school I rarely start drinking, but sometimes I do. "It's five o'clock in the ocean," I jokingly tell myself as I make my first "small one," of the day.

By the time my husband is home from work for the day I usually have dinner ready and another small drink with my dinner. Fast forward to bedtime and the chance my husband and I are finally able to unwind together from our chaotic days. He settles in with his second drink of the day, I on my third. We both consume 3-4 alcoholic drinks almost every single night of the week. Maybe we aren't so bad as opposed to the real alcoholics. My gastroenterologist sees me regularly because of my chronic gastritis and he asks me how I could possibly have so much inflammation. I shrug and say that I have no idea, maybe I eat too much spicy food. Again, with the lies and the alcohol abuse and the numbing, I cannot go on like this, it really fucking stinks.

Oh, and speaking of stinks, have you ever smelled a sack of rotting potatoes? I could never quite place my finger on the scent that lingered in any room that my mom entered. I don't know if it was a disorder or her lack of self-care but she had a scent to her that I can now only describe as rotting potatoes, urine, fish, and smoke. Oddly comforting to me and I would give anything to bury myself in her hugs.

My signature scent has consisted of a mix between lavender, patchouli, Burberry perfume, weed, cigarettes, and alcohol. I have dropped the last two within the past five years. The first time I visited New York I was twenty years old. I rode up in a van with four other people. I was a last-minute tag along but was still expected to pay fully for the hotel. I never did get to pay them back. I hardly even used the hotel honestly. My acquaintances were all four visiting colleges on that trip, and I was just tagging along to see the sights solo in NYC. I started drinking the moment we left and didn't really stop until we were on the way back home a couple days later. My friends were legally allowed to drink, and I was not. So, I stayed back at the hotel by myself and drank alone.

The maintenance man came up to the hotel room around midnight or so, I couldn't get the remote to work so I called the front desk asking for assistance. He kindly helped me fix the TV and I asked him if he wanted to take a shot with me. He agreed. After we had a drink and introduced ourselves, I asked what he was up to because I was bored and lonely and felt like I could use a friend as all of mine were out in an unfamiliar city together. He then let me follow him around to the basement where we would eat snacks and watch the fresh prince of bel air. It was roughly 3am at this point and he told me that he had to start preparing the continental breakfast ready for the hotel guests. I asked if he could use any help and he said he could. After helping him stock muffins and pop tarts, pull back the curtains and brew the coffee, we shook hands and hugged and I thanked him for letting me follow him around.

I went back up to the hotel room where I found my friends had drunkenly passed out. The big dude I was supposed to bunk with had taken up three fourths of the bed and was snoring louder than any human should ever be capable of. I could not sleep in these conditions. I took another shot from the bottle we had in our room and decided to walk around NYC alone at 4:30AM. I walked down to find the studio that was at the time filming "Good Morning America," and after looking so ridiculously desperate the staff opened their doors and let me on the set. I was drunk and sleep deprived on Good

Morning America, in my fake blonde wig, smeared red lipstick, and cat footie pajamas. Jamie Fox was the guest star in the studio that day and I was able to snap a photo of myself with him during this ridiculous time in my life. The woman standing directly behind me stated that someone close to her reeked of alcohol. I wasn't even embarrassed, I was just happy to be in front of the cameras. Starring in my own television reality show.

New York has never felt comfortable for me but Los Angeles has always had my heart. From the first time visiting LA for America's Next Top Model, to the last time I was in California visiting a best friend of mine in Pasadena. My six-hour plane ride from the east to west coast was full of anxiety and caffeine. This was the first time I would be leaving my child for more than 24 hours and I couldn't handle the heart ache. I tried to sleep on the plane but I typically like to chase my anxiety with a bottle of insomnia, so I was wide awake and full of regret. I have also acquired a fear of flying in my old age so that didn't help the matter. I know that my husband is a good dad and he knows what he is doing but I couldn't shake the fear that what if I would never see them again. My son ended up having a high fever while I was away and my friend rubbed my back as I was bawling on the phone with his PCP, hundreds of miles away. Having my son saved my life and now I was abandoning him in my eyes. I cannot abandon my children, I will be better. He was just a few months over two years old and my husband and I had already been trying for six months to give our only child a sibling. I was mad and I regretted my decision to go on the plane because at the time of my trip to visit my friend I was ovulating and we would be forgoing that enter cycle for me to go on this trip. However, I was very happy to be with my best friend since we were in high school. She had been there by my side through some really shitty boyfriends and even shittier times. We were both dating boys that were also friends when we were just out of high school so our dating dynamic worked really well.

My husband and I tried for nearly nine months before we found out we would be expecting a sibling for our two-year-old. After seeing a fertility specialist for a couple of months I underwent a procedure that showed one of my fallopian tubes was totally blocked. Ah, so we really were just rolling the dice not even knowing if ovulating was even happening for me during those nine months. The nurse told me that I would be extremely fertile after that procedure, and she was 100% right. We conceived our second child during that cycle and after I had finally stopped trying so hard. There is peace in letting go of your control in making things "just so," and letting life happen with you as a part of it. I woke my husband up the morning I found out I was pregnant, and he was annoyed that I didn't just wait until he woke up for work. I was so excited, but I felt like I was the only one that wanted that moment and I will never have a moment like that again. My third child was a surprise. The excitement factor was not there until much later. My first child was a surprise baby conceived even through monthly birth control pills. Apparently my bi-polar medication was making the birth control less effective. I have wanted to have one of those exciting, "how do I tell the husband," moments and it was ruined. I woke him up wearing a shirt that said, "I am so pregnant," thinking I would have a cute YouTube moment. I am starting this new year with no expectations in hopes that maybe I won't need moments like these to feel happiness or validation. If I can only let go of my expectations maybe I can see the world for what it is, an endless chaotic series of circumstances and chances.

I was never a very heavy smoker but I did smoke more than a pack of cigarettes weekly for roughly ten years off and on. The day that my husband and I found out that we were expecting our first child was coincidentally the day I ran out of my pack of cigarettes. My husband said that was it and I wouldn't be smoking anymore, and I agreed because smoking when you're pregnant is so tacky. I found out that I was pregnant at roughly four weeks, my cycle was like clockwork, so I knew when things weren't on routine. For nine weeks following that positive pregnancy test I continued to smoke cigarettes here and there and eventually would smoke cloves that contained no nicotine in order to taper off from smoking cigarettes. I would hide behind my work, and I would smoke a cigarette and eat a shitty, greasy, slice of 711 pizza before going back inside the building of my work where I worked as a receptionist at a holistic doctor's office. I was a fraud, but I was so used to hiding secrets that it really didn't even matter to me, this was my nature. Lying and hiding and running away from my problems was how I lived for 22 years so how was I going to just stop that cold turkey?

My mom used to tell me and her friends and family that I lived in a fantasy world. She was right though, I think that I did live in make believe for most of my life. I had no limits, no rules, nothing holding me back from dreaming and acting on my dreams. I was in a fantasy world where no one and nothing could hurt me, I was invincible. For 22 years I lived as though I was floating between actual reality and reality television episodes that I would star in. Where do I fit in here and how on earth am I going to fake it until I make it. There were times in my life that I built relationships with men on the internet and with no fear, no rules, nothing saving me from myself, I would meet them in person.

I truly am very lucky to be alive because for a lot of other people that may have done half of the same stupid things that I have, well they are not here to tell there stories. They are not here to show their silly tattoos that were done by an amateur in Iowa. I have even ridden in a car with a complete stranger for eighteen hours because we were both in Florida at the same time and I needed to get home due to an unmedicated manic episode. He was a pretty well-known local photographer in the same city that I was living in and I was stuck in Florida having a panic attack with no money and no way back home. I was able to reach out to him just minutes before my cell phone died and he picked me up at the location I gave him, no questions asked. We then drove the eighteen hours back home together and it didn't feel weird or creepy at all to me. I'm pretty sure he ended up having a crush on me as he took me out for my twenty-first birthday, but he was a decade older than I was and I was not about that life when I was 20. Something I used to pride myself on was my ability to read people and their potential intentions, but I failed at that a lot too.

I was twenty years old and living with my mother and brother when I accidentally attended a rave. Some acquaintances I knew messaged me on a social media platform and let me know that he and some of his friends would be going camping in my area. He lived about an hour and a half from me and I needed someone to buy my alcohol as I ran out. I asked if he would buy me booze, he and his friends offered for me to go camping with them. Then I packed my bookbag along with my blanket and pillow, an outfit, and my cell phone charger. I walked and met him and his friend with my belongings at the liquor store a half a mile from my home. My friend bought the booze he said he would and we headed out for the mountains. When we arrived at the RAVE I was pretty dumbfounded but figured oh that's alright I can adjust to this new development. The weather was much colder than I expected, and my thin blanket hardly kept me lukewarm. The music was so loud my bones felt like they were going to vibrate out of my skin. So many new smells and new drugs all around me but I had never felt so alone and out of my element before. I needed an escape, and I didn't know how or why but I am still here to tell this weird ass story.

My phone quickly dwindled its battery life as I had been talking to a boy I was previously dating the entire time I was camping. There was not a single place that I could charge my cell phone and everyone I was with didn't seem to care. I abandoned my belongings and my friends and decided I would just walk until someone would find me. I was passing people that were passed out against their cars in the tall grass. I passed homes that looked as though no one had lived there for years even though there were obvious signs of humans living there currently. I didn't really have a plan, I just needed to get out of the situation quickly because it didn't feel right. Through some act of something beyond myself I was found walking by my boyfriend at the time. It felt like I had walked a half of a day before I saw his familiar face. We didn't talk much as he drove me back to my home with my mom and brother. I was truly exhausted emotionally and physically and I was still trying to figure out what I had just been through the past 24 hours.

Thirty years old now and I still have no clue who I want to be or what I want to do when I grow up. I do not even consider myself to be grown up even though I have been an adult now for over a decade. The more adults I talk to about this, the more I see that I am not alone and there are a lot of us that still haven't found our niche. My moods change by the minute some days and my hobbies follow suit. I believe the first career I wanted to have as a child was to be an actress. I was successful in some ways as I was on a reality television show, in addition to one HBO show, and one Netflix show. Never the star of a real movie but playing the part as if I was in my own real life. After an aptitude test in elementary school revealed that the only career, I would ever have would be the life of a clown I knew I had to do some internal digging. That's the year my mother booked me a special birthday gift as a copilot at the local airport. The pilot let me take control so that's when I decided that when I was grown up I would be a pilot. Also, the year I discovered that I was afraid of heights, so I slowly let my pilot dreams take a nosedive.

Okay so, I guess I wouldn't be an actress, and I guess I wouldn't be a pilot, I loved food, eating was something I was very good at as a kid. Way before I let my eating disorder rob me of living, I enjoyed eating just as much as I enjoyed cooking. There was even a time when I was nineteen that I toyed with the idea of being an exotic dancer. I asked for an application at the strip club one night with my friends, which apparently there is no application, you just go and "try out," one night. So, I drove thirty minutes to the strip club and I chugged a bottle of booze that I brought with me. I awkwardly danced with another woman and as she clearly was telling me to get a life, I went to the far corner of the stage to attempt to dance solo. Yet again, this was another time that I was unsuccessful in my life. I fell on my eight-dollar high heels and on my clothed, boney, bulimic, ass. A big stripper fail of mine is that I wouldn't take off all of my clothes, that's a pretty big requirement in the industry apparently. Some dude in a checkered, white and blue button up handed me four one-dollar bills and I said thanks and took it. That four dollars paid for my gas to and from my two-hour long career as an exotic dancer.

I am now a stay-at-home chef, taxi driver, nurse, and butler for my family of five and I love it. Something inside of me lights up when my family is happy with something that I have cooked for them. I will gladly make all our meals as long as it keeps them smiling with full bellies and fuller hearts. Being someone's mom or even someone's wife is not something I ever even considered to be in my future. I make no money, I clean up messes that I didn't make, I wipe assess that aren't my own, and I clean dried boogers off the wall that I didn't put there. Truly I wouldn't change my life in any single way. Constantly reminding myself that I have been in such dark places and this light inside of me that has grown a family has been there to light my way as I am navigating this journey of motherhood.

I don't believe that fear is something you are born with but instead fear slowly seeps in as you grow and see the world for every crack and imperfection. My fears have been just as bipolar as the rest of me, changing day to day. However, my fear of death and losing one of my children keeps me in a constant hyperactive anxious state. My mom used to tell me that she hadn't had a good night's sleep since before my sister was born. I assumed in my arrogance, that as your children age the less anxious you will be and the more sleep you will get. They are constantly growing and learning without a true sense of fear which is absolutely terrifying. My husband and I joke that we will sleep again in eighteen years, but I think we both know that isn't true. There will always be new fears and continually smarter children as they grow and change and adapt to their world. Their generation is going to change the world and I am so thrilled to be a part of it. I still do not really feel qualified to be someone's mother, but I am so glad that I was offered this position.

Tonight is one of those cold, windy, January mornings and I can feel her in every bending branch. The pine trees bring us nothing but mosquitoes in the summertime but right now in our winter, I can feel my mother's arms wrap around me with every gust of wind. Her ashes are in an urn sitting next to a clock we received as a wedding gift. My children think it's just so neat that Nana is always here with them. So much so that during a playdate with some of their friends and their parents, my child told his friend that we keep nana in a jar. I imagine that little boy probably thought at that time that my son was either lying or that we were a family of serial killers. My mom did what she thought was best for us and I never really thanked her until she was dying. During her last year and after her accident, her memories were even more fuzzy than they normally were for her. She would get so upset and end up crying and apologizing to me for the life we had as children. The doctors had her on a half a dozen different medications for pain and anxiety. Some days she would be the bitchy mother I always knew and loved and other days she was someone's nana, she was a much better nana.

Impatiently patient,
Legs dangling from your chair,
Hands up high, high in the air,
Screaming that no one is there,
No, no one cares,
I've found a handful of four leaf clovers,

But here I am still fucking you over.

It was difficult for my husband to connect with my mother because he saw her for what she did to me. From the early stages of our relationship, she just never wore well on him. There was one time that my mom had even called my boyfriend because she said I was missing, and she couldn't find me anywhere in our home. She panicked and contacted everyone that she knew of who talked to me including my boyfriend before she would contact the police. I was living in the basement of our rancher, and I just did not hear her call down to me that morning because I was most likely still blacked out from drinking too much the previous night. Drinking to the point of blacking out was the one thing I was really good at and it never abandoned me.

After I moved in with my boyfriend, he proposed, we got married and then quickly became pregnant, my mother was still hurting me. There were times when I was pregnant with our first child that my mom would call me to yell at me and call me a bitch, or a whore. My husband hated when she did this to me, he felt defenseless. After our first child was born my mom threatened to take my husband and I to court with a 10 page letter stating how unfit we were as parents and how she would have our son taken away from us. She stated in the letter that we were out partying every weekend and leaving our baby to go do so. False. She also said in the letter that she would fight for her grandparent visitation rights. Also false. There is no such thing as "grandparent visitation rights," in our state. It was very difficult for my husband to connect and sympathize with my mother in her last year following her accident and eventually her time with hospice and her death. I truly do not blame him for that one bit.

My small, black, heart breaks a little more each time that someone is cruel to me or I feel rejected or criticized in any way. I have worked very hard to climb up this ladder of acceptance and positivity, one that I have built by myself with no tools and no instructions to follow. When I know in my heart that I am being kind or doing the right thing and someone yells at me or hurts my feelings I instantly go into fight mode. I have felt the need to defend myself from a very early age not necessarily in a physical defense, but I had to defend my emotions. No one can know you like you know yourself and I am tired of trying to justify my emotional needs and well-being. You try and you try and when all you have left to do is try and even that goes overlooked, you think that you have to defend your reasoning to keep moving forward. I will forgive myself for always being so self-critical. We all have a different idea of what success means and it is so important to remind myself that I need to let go of these standards. I set my expectations so high when my sister and I were kids and would fantasize about our adult lives because we needed that escape. I make these daily lists and I count my quota for the day, just hoping I won't get bored or fired from this position that I have graciously accepted.

The truth is that I have held many different jobs and some of them I worked two at a time. My first job was as a cashier at a fast-food chain. I was 15 years old, and it was also the summer I started to drink alcohol and smoke cigarettes. My dad was so proud of me for starting out in the workforce at such a young age, I was even promoted to train new employees and I was not even sixteen years old yet. Of course, my step mom would always tell us about how she started working when she was thirteen. My entire life has been spent achieving something or being diagnosed with some illness and then someone in my family one-upping me. When I had my heart issues as a child, my mom stated that she had the same thing. When I found out I had my brain condition, my family panicked because it has been known to be hereditary. Just a few months after my first son was born, a new boy was on the way in my family. I know that I am not a big important person or special in any way, but can't I just have one thing? If I have a new condition, so does everyone else. Am I spreading like wildfire, am I spreading my own plague? How can I turn this around and into something positive? I am learning to let this light inside of me come out all around me in hopes that everyone will catch it. Please let this warmth inside my small, black, heart infect my family.

One of the hardest things about having a mental disorder is feeling the need to explain your feelings to those who love you. There are times I cannot stay too long at a cookout or a family gathering because something triggers me, and I let the PTSD consume me. From there I become openly agitated and look like a huge bitch, when I really just need to leave the situation and remind myself that the past has made me who I am today. I try to explain to my family about my many coats of mental illnesses, shedding my skin to admit my faults and I go in one ear and out the other. I try not to fault anyone who doesn't understand mental illness, but I do fault those who aren't willing to educate themselves on the matter. My mom grew up in an age where mental illness was just summed up as being crazy, and if you are biologically a woman, then it must be your time of the month if you're, "extra crazy." It really isn't fair to call someone with a mental illness crazy, whether their mental illnesses are due to a malfunction in their brain, or the way that they were raised. And if you're super lucky like me, then you have a mental disorder because of both of these factors.

In the summer after my second child was born, I started experiencing this extreme pain throughout both legs and down my lower back. The pain in my legs was so bad that I would cry myself to sleep only to be woken a few hours later in more pain. After scheduling an appointment with my primary care physician, she decided to run some routine blood work to see if we could figure out what was causing me to have so much pain. The day following the blood draw I received a phone call from the nurse I saw just two days before and she told me that I tested positive for Lyme disease. Lyme disease, really? I only remember ever having a tick on me twice in my lifetime. The first time I found a tick on me was in fifth grade and it was the Monday following a daddy weekend. We must have been outside a lot on that daddy weekend as we often were as children. I was in my fifth-grade reading class and I put my hair behind my left ear only to feel a new bump that was not there previously. I quickly ripped off the bump and raised my hand to ask the teacher if I could use the restroom. I ran to the bathroom with this black bump in my hands quickly shutting the stall behind me to lock it. Oh no what was this thing, were my sci-fi worms back? I wrapped the black dot in toilet paper and flushed it down the toilet. The second time I remember having a tick on me was when I was eighteen years old. My boyfriend at the time and I were in his room after being out all day with our friends. We were in his room and after making out, he took off my pants and there was a tick crawling up my leg. Mood killed, tick smashed.

After finding out that I had Lyme disease I was shoved into doctors' offices only for them to tell me that I did not in fact have Lyme disease, even though my bloodwork was positive. The infectious disease doctor told me that because I was a young mother of two children I was just stressed out and that was causing me to have so many medical issues and I guess many positive blood tests too. Pro tip: if you ever test positive for Lyme disease do not ever see an infectious disease doctor.

I was frustrated and in so much pain with no doors to turn and knock on. Through my local community I have been able to connect with other individuals that also have chronic Lyme disease and some day I hope to get rid of this illness completely. Between my pregnancies and my time nursing my babies I have not had the chance to receive the proper treatment for Lyme disease. I also do not have the funds to be able to see a Lyme literate doctor in regards to treating me. The first Lyme literate doctor I saw charges patients out of pocket and does not use insurance companies as he caters more to the Mennonite community. He had me tested through a few different blood tests that cost my family eight hundred dollars out of pocket. I haven't been back since. The second Lyme literate doctor I saw was quite helpful until I found out about my brain condition, Chiari malformation. Unfortunately, she is no longer in practice. For those individuals that do have Lyme disease then you can understand the financial struggle and burden that you must carry day to day. For those of you who do not know, there is a huge controversy within the CDC over Lyme disease and its importance as well as treatment methods. I encourage you to do some digging in the Lyme disease and CDC controversy, it really is fascinating to learn about.

I saw my primary care physician last week after asking her to increase my anti depression medication. My five food groups are coffee, water, Zoloft, taco bell, and pizza. It's truly amazing that I have made it to my thirties. My husband drew me a picture when we were dating, of my five food groups and it's still in my bed side table drawer. "Intermittent fasting," is the new socially acceptable way to admit that you have an eating disorder by disguising it as a fad diet. I shamefully admit that I haven't been really eating as much as I should be according to my chart height and weight. Whether it is a side effect from increasing my depression medication or my mania is too manic with all of the extra caffeine I have been feeding to it. My mom was always on some diet as I was growing up. Which as I realize now is a little strange because she was medically considered to be overweight for her charted height. She was self-medicating with junk food, alcohol, and cigarettes in the evening and during the day she would just drink sparkling water and decaf coffee. Looking back, I see now just how alike she and I really were, if only we could have opened up about ourselves a little bit better. Maybe then I wouldn't dream of her being alive every single night. I'm not sure if I would consider my dreams of her in fact dreams, or rather terrible nightmares. My doctor has recently recommended a medication that is given to patients with PTSD to help lessen their night terrors. He said that the medication was intended for patients with high blood pressure and because my blood pressure is often lower than the norm, I would have a difficult time getting out of bed the following morning after taking it because I would be extremely dizzy. No thanks doc, I'd rather pretend that I can still see her when in fact all that I can see is her black and beige urn sitting next to our grandfather clock.

In need of a pack of gum and gasoline for our car, my children and I went to the local grocery store. We were in and out of the store in a miraculous six minutes. One disabled mom and two toddlers in and out of a grocery store in six minutes, let that sink in. I strapped the children into their designated seats and buckled myself in as I adjusted the rear-view mirror and switched the gear from park to reverse. There was an elderly man in the handicap spot beside the handicap spot that I was backing up from. He looked at me and then he looked at the handicap sign sticking out of the ground in the parking spot that I had just left with my two toddlers. I pressed the button on my driver's side door to allow the passenger side window to go down. My kids and I were laughing about something silly and I had a big smile on my face when I asked the man if there was a problem. He asked why I was parked in a handicap spot. I was speechless as I removed my temporary handicap tag to show the man that I was given temporary handicap parking as I had major surgery on my driving foot just a couple of months prior. The pain I continue to feel daily whether from the surgical site or from the bone spur growing back is something I am not sure of, but for some reason I had to explain to this elderly man why a young female such as myself is disabled. Why do I have to explain to anyone in front of my children why I have disabilities? I would never ever ask someone in a handicap parking space why they are handicap. I told the man to please not judge me so harshly as I drove away with tears streaming down my face explaining to my toddlers why mommy was crying. I wanted to call my mom to tell her about the awful man I encountered and how I tried to be brave and handle the situation without getting my little black heart involved. But then I remembered that the last time I tried to call her cellphone to just hear her voice on her voicemail recording her number had finally been dropped by the cell phone company. For many months following her accident and then her death I would call her cell phone just in order to hear her raspy voicemail recording but now that was gone too.

Sleep was always difficult for me to reach

when I was growing up, so much so that I would down my thoughts in bottles of booze so I would just black out and choose not to have any more thoughts. I will now drink a mug of sleepy tea with honey after the kids go to bed. It's a gamble when I fall asleep because I don't know which part of my PTSD is alive and thriving in my own subconscious. Is it my mother, my childhood, my abandonment issues, my narcissistic first love, my intimacy issues, my jealousy issues, my anger issues, etc. Half of my life I have found a way to self-medicate in a bottle that was not medically prescribed so that I would not have to feel the trauma again in a nightmare. Maybe I will talk to that doctor about the nightmare medication, maybe it is okay to dream again. I grew up thinking that PTSD was something that only soldiers could have and therefore you were a warrior if you were able to live through it. Although I have never fought for our country, I have fought my own battles, and given myself a freedom I never knew existed, and for that I am a warrior. I will continue to fight these battles within my own thoughts sometimes daily if I have to because even though I have been through some shit, I want to see what's going to happen next.

Now that I am aware of almost all of my medical conditions, I have an entire team that follows me annually to ensure that I am staying healthy. Podiatrist, dentist, physical therapist, cardiologist, geneticist, neurologist, gastroenterologist, dermatologist, neurosurgeon, allergist, and lastly my PCP. This is the year I found out that I am allergic to just about everything in the world, which is related to my mast cell activation syndrome which coincides with my connective tissue disorder, Ehlers Danlos syndrome. Still questioning that higher power as to how I survived as a zygote. Most of my medical conditions are related to a hiccup in my genetic make-up, so maybe I really am a sci-fi star. Will I be the next x-woman? That'd be neat. It is extremely difficult to advocate for yourself in the medical world when you are practically screaming for someone to listen to you. As a woman, I believe it is twice as difficult for us. My mom started seeing a therapist roughly a year before her accident. After all the years of her telling my sister and I to be strong and independent women, she finally admitted that she needed help. There is nothing wrong with reaching out to someone if you need help, there is something wrong if you are just trying to self-medicate and ignore things on your own. It takes a village and there is absolutely no need to carry such heavy burdens alone.

Last night I slept for just under thirteen hours straight floating between ptsd nightmares and hopeful futuristic dreams. There will always be two sides to who I am and that is something that I will eventually have to forgive myself for. The timeline is simple, there is who I was and what I went through before my mother's accident and there's who I am and what I will go through after my mother's accident. I never realized just how much a death can change a person until it happened. Where have I been this past year? Am I still in our duplex across from the bank that was robbed monthly? In my closet hangs a black three-quarter length blouse. It is a very soft almost silky fabric with even darker black polka dots all around the blouse. I have only worn this blouse one time and I doubt I will ever wear it again. It's my death shirt, everyone has a death outfit. It's that all black dress or all black suit that you only wear to viewings and funerals. Mine is a designer brand quarter length polka dot shirt that I wore to my mother's memorial service. Do I dare wear this ominous clothing again? No way, will I instead donate it? That will also be a hard no. I cannot burden anyone else with my black heart, death outfit. It will hang and collect dust and lint until the next time I have to wear such a burden.

In writing this book I have gained so much of my life back that I never knew existed. My mother was so mentally sick that when my sister was in sixth grade and I was in fourth grade, she begged our father to let us live with him for one month and so we did. She could not handle being a mentally ill, unmedicated single mother. This was before she got knocked-up by my brother's father. This was before she threatened to take all three of our lives in her red jeep liberty unless I chose to live with her. I often wondered why my own mom hated me so much, why couldn't she just be happy like everyone else's mom? Why couldn't my mom be a cookie cutting, apron wearing, suburban single mom? She was unknowingly starring in the film of my life as the villian when, spoiler alert, she was not truly a villain at all, she was just very very ill. I wonder who this woman could have been if she only sought help for her mental health illnesses sooner, maybe our relationship would have been better. Then I jump to the thoughts of myself not being enough for anyone, so selfish of me. Who would I have been if I made better friends in high school and didn't get caught up in alcohol? I could have been someone good.

I am average height, average weight, average appearance, average personality, and average energy level for someone my age. I will not wake up with a beautifully warm smile on my face every morning to greet the sun every single day. That's just not who I am, I have never really been much of a morning person. My children never asked me if I was a morning person or not so every other day I had to be. My husband and I are a team and everything we do is 50/50 which I believe is extremely important in a relationship. He will wake up with our children at five AM on a Monday and I will wake up at 5:05 AM on the following Tuesday. We will exchange I love you's and stale coffee breath kisses as he rushes out the door off to work for the day. I remain in my pajamas until I have to leave the house again which really isn't often unless we forget something at the grocery store which is often. He is dapper and charming as he waves goodbye to his family and parts with them for the day. Am I enough for him? Will he find someone better between now and 4:30pm? I am bruised and broken, definitely not a morning person, never suzy sunshine, not a night owl either really, barely a people person, I now have white highlights from aging. He will find someone better than me and I am sure of it in my tiny black heart. Please don't take my sunshine away, please let the good one stay.

I never wanted to be one of those jealous wife types. I don't like to assume and snoop and feel highly insecure while doing so. Instead, I will be better than what my brain is telling me. Around 3pm every day I freshen myself up with a hairstyle, fresh makeup, and a new spray of my favorite burberry perfume. Maybe if he comes home to a clean house, a pretty wife, and a warm meal, maybe then he won't leave. My husband never expects these things from me, I just assume I have to do these things in order for my significant other to not cheat. It's the way society projects stay at home wife/mother types to be. From being bulimic, anorexic, alcoholic, and desperate weighing in at 105lbs, my husband loved me. To weigh 170lbs when I was pregnant with our first son, no makeup, and very gassy, my husband loved me. Through my slurred vows to my positive pregnancy tests have remained by my side and he has loved me. I do not deserve the unconditional love that he gives my tiny black heart or so I am conditioned to believe. I will be a better person and it is mostly because my husband has opened my heart and my eyes. My oldest son has a therapy appointment for some anger issues he has been having. He saw a therapist because he is just like his mother with his deep questions at seven years old. "Mommy, why are we here?" I don't know how to answer him.

When taking my son back to school after his therapy session we parked in the student drop off parking. He was late as I promised him we would get a new watch for him to be able to tell the time whenever he wanted, even if that meant every five minutes he would tell me what time it was. I parked our car and unloaded all of the children and made sure that I had the doctor's notice from the therapist to excuse his absence. We had to be buzzed in by the front desk staff at his primary school. The secretary asked who was returning to school and I told her my son's name and handed her his doctor's note. As we were discussing the new system of picking up and dropping off students with their high tech ID scanner, a student slipped out of the front door. He ran to our gray SUV that was parked in the student drop off parking and yanked hard on the door handle in an attempt to open the car door. The secretary ran outside screaming for assistance from other primary school staff as she tried to help the autistic boy back inside the building. I only mention his autism as I was hoping to be able to offer my calm self to the secretary for possible aid in the situation. The secretary was obviously very flustered over this so I ran out of the front door of the school with my infant in my arms. I yelled to the boy, "Hey buddy, would you like to come read with me and the baby." That was enough distraction for the school staff to help the secretary get the boy back inside the primary school safely. I grabbed the shoulders of the secretary and I said to her, "Hey it's okay, he's safe now," and I gave her a friendly hug. Maybe this little black heart really is growing.

I never knew that skin picking was a self-destructive habit until my therapist told me so. I have been digging my nails into my skin for as long as I can remember. Mostly on my hairline because you can't see the scabs that way. I'd hate to shave my head to see the scars that lie underneath my thick brown, but graying hair. Picking scabs, and even warts as a teenager is just something I have always done to cope with my anxiety, I didn't know it was considered self-harm. The boy I dated as a teenager and young adult used to yank my hand away from wherever it was that I was picking. Like training a dog I suppose, he would rub my nose in the scabs and make me learn my lesson. I was to wear what clothes he wanted me to wear and to do my hair as it pleased him. He picked me up from my mother's apartment once and we went off driving to spend the day together. I pulled down the vanity mirror in his car from the passenger seat as I was going to touch up my makeup for the day. He told me I was prettier without it and threw my makeup box out the window of his moving car. Yes, master I will do as you please. I lived for so long being manipulated and trained in my obedience that I felt silenced as if I had no say in what would happen in my life. How could I break this dog chain that I was being choked and dragged with? My control was found in the secrets of my addictions, my confidence was found in the lies I told. Barely able to stand, I was being held together as if I was a broken porcelain doll, my addictions and my lies held me together like glue.

My mom, my sister, and I always spent girl time together before my brother was born. We had nights that we set aside for the girls or crafts that would be made together with girl power and elbow grease. There were afternoons that we would spend together at a ceramics shop, picking out the ceramic figurine we would one by one select, we would paint and polish them and for that day, they meant so much to us. My mom never kept many things and truly she was a hoarder of candy wrappers and diet caffeine free soda cans, more than she was a hoarder of monumental memories like the ceramics. In every apartment, town house, duplex, single family home my mother ever had, she left behind her mark on the walls, and memories in the crawl space. I have almost no photos of being an infant, a child, or of any art I made for my mom. I have no baby clothes that she has saved for me coming home from the hospital, or no family heirlooms that my mom held on to, to pass down to generations.

There are drawers in my home that are full to the brim of my children's artwork, dentist appointment receipts, scribbles on napkins, etc. Afraid of letting the little things leave me so I hold on to them as I would have clung to my own baby box if I had one. So badly I wish I could talk to my mom again and ask her if she had a storage unit, or anywhere that she would have kept my life with her. Deep down I know that no such place exists. She packed up and moved her home frequently when I was growing up, no time to take each memory with her. Instead, I can rely on the remaining family members of my mother's family that still talk to me and the few photos I have in which we are all smiling and laughing. What a fraud.

A photo is worth a thousand words, but we didn't grow up with silver spoons in our mouths. Rather we grew up with disposable plastic wear and paper plates. There were documented photos that I can visually remember of the apartment we lived in as children with our mother. Dishes would be collecting crust and flies as they were seen towering well above the sink. Every other square in the ceiling held one of those long sticky paper fly traps and they were completely covered with dead flies. Some were still buzzing as if to scream to one of their dead cousins to put them out of their misery. We didn't grow up with a dishwasher but instead we washed our dishes by hand, actually we didn't wash them. Our kitchen sink became a biohazard and the kitchen floor, a breathing ground for bacteria. She never dusted our home which is most likely why I have an allergy to dust as an adult. The only times I remember my mother actually cleaning the home is when she knew that CPS or the landlord would be coming by for a spot check. All they would do is peek their head in to give our apartment a god, "once over." If only they would have looked behind the doors at the piles of trash and old food. My father paid my mother monthly child support in order for his daughters to thrive but instead he was just feeding his ex-wife's self-medicating addictions unknowingly.

The day of my husband and I's wedding was a cold afternoon in early November. My husband and I paid for our wedding ourselves so we were looking for the cheapest alternative for everything. Venue wise we decided to get married in my mom's rented backyard of her home at the time. As always before a major event, my mom cleaned her home, but little hints of her illness were throughout her home. The big, white, fridge held months old gallons of whole milk with that fat and the water clearly separated. An iceberg sized chunk of rotten milk floating around in a plastic carton next to some fruit and veggie trays for our wedding guests. She had two bathrooms in her rented rancher, one had a bathtub that didn't work and the other had a toilet that didn't flush. My brother still had the same bedroom as he did when I still lived with them, only now he had a mini fridge. My youngest brother was twelve years old when I married my husband. Inside of my brother's mini fridge held roughly the same contents as the main fridge. He had week old sandwich meat and rotting cheese in one big lump layer of mold. I was so happy to be leaving that world behind, drunkenly saying my I dos and choosing a life of happiness. I can do this because I will be better.

My children prefer to stay home in the comfort of their familiarity and family rather than to travel outside of the home. My little, cold, black, heart has been so warmed through the eyes of my children. I never wanted to be home, it was so cold and dark, I hated living in the shadows. All I wanted was for someone to see me and help me escape this life. My husband sparked a light inside of me that had never been lit before and since my little black heart has started to warm up, there is no going back. I will continue to push forward and to keep climbing because I know now that I am capable of warmth and love even if I was grown up believing the opposite. We joke that our children love us so much and that is why they like to wake up well before 6AM most days, they just want to be with us. I wonder what it feels like to love your home and your parents so much that you actually want to be with them and love them. Perhaps they are spoiled but the way I see it is the world is a cruel, dark place at times and I want them to always have the love and warmth to come home to.

My life has been spent unwillingly participating in a constant ballet of sit down, stand up, smile more, close your mouth, dress this way, straighten your hair, never able to cut myself loose of what held me back. Sitting on our family room couch I can see from my seat that our home alarm system is set to the armed for stay setting. The home that I grew up in had its own rigged alarm system. The big, red, front door was locked and that felt pretty safe, however, the hideaway key was always in a simple place that even a monkey could find. On top of that my sister and I would lose the hideaway keys often, so we kept our ground level windows unlocked. The basement did not have outside access but did offer access through the enclosed back porch. Our back entrance of the house was a big white door that was always broken and never locked so instead of having someone come and fix it, my mom and her husband had a small, black, chair propped up against the handle of the golden back doorknob. It was our west side avenue alarm system and even though the local bank directly across the street from us was robbed almost monthly, we were never robbed. We never had much to offer, but thankfully that small, black, chair held together well for our broken family of five.

The day before my mom had left her physical body on this plain, she began to become more noticeably ill. Ever since the night of her accident I had researched and researched until my eyes were red from insomnia. I looked up everything I could possibly find on spinal cord injuries, brain injuries, incomplete spinal cord injury, life threatening injury, quadriplegic, etc. My mom had three children and my older sister and younger brother were both on my mom's paperwork for power of attorney. My name was not. I knew from early on how severe her injury was and how little hope I had of her full recovery because of everything I read about. Unless you can tend to a spinal cord injury in a timely manner, then the likelihood of her having a full or close to full recovery wasn't as high. She had been lying on the carpet between her attic steps and her bedroom for roughly six hours before she was found. Once first responders were on the scene, that itself took about an hour trying to figure out how to get her out of the inhuman position she was in. The ambulance ride to the nearest hospital took twenty minutes and once there she was at that hospital for roughly an hour before the hospital staff decided that they weren't as well equipped as another hospital nearby that was also a teaching hospital. Now it had been close to nine hours since her traumatic fall and the flying conditions weren't recommended due to the harsh march wind. She was then taken by ambulance to a teaching hospital in another state that was an hour and a half from where she was currently lying. Almost twelve hours had passed before my mom received the proper medical care needed for her life-threatening injury. I read that the three biggest reasons for death to occur following a spinal cord injury are pneumonia, blood clots, and bed sores.

Three months passed since her spinal cord and brain injury and we were told that our mom would be placed in a rehab facility in order to get strong enough to coordinate her useless limbs for occupational therapy. She was rushed to the hospital many times during those first three months which we were told was likely to happen. A few days before my husband and I went on a summer vacation with his family my mother coded twice in the ICU. I was visiting her one of those times. I sat with her and asked her to either be strong or let go because her fight was a big one and I wanted her to make that decision. I was told that she was awake the prior evening asking nurses for a gun to kill herself. While holding her hand in the ICU I watched her pulse ox drop, drop, drop faster than I could catch my own breath. I felt as if I was whispering to the nurses to suit up in their biohazard gear in order to enter her isolation chambers to come save my mother. At this point so early on in her injury recovery, she was not listed as "DNR," (do not resuscitate.) The nurses came quickly to suction my mother's trach tube in order for her oxygen to come back quickly into her sad lungs. She often got pneumonia during her last year with us, I blamed her habitual heavy smoking. I used to sneak into her bedroom when I was a teenager in order to steal a half-smoked butt from her ashtray on her bedside table, but she always smoked them all the way down to the filter so my attempts were never fulfilled.

I started smoking cigarettes in the summer before I turned sixteen years old. The first cigarette I ever smoked was a Newport menthol blend. A friend of mine had a pack and she gave me one to try out. After smoking the entire Newport all the way down to the butt rather quickly just like mom, I had to sit down on the grassy hill because my head felt so light and everything around me was spinning so fast. Before quitting cigarettes in May 2015, I smoked two to three packs of cigarettes a week. My mom smoked in every single home she ever rented. So much so that when we were evicted or chose to move elsewhere, the silhouette of where a painting was once hung was outlined with gray smoke stains.

I often wonder if perhaps my mom didn't smoke so much that maybe her lungs wouldn't have failed her so much after her accident. Well before my mom moved to Cumberland she would have bronchitis almost weekly it seemed. There wasn't a phone conversation with her that I don't remember her coughing through the entire thing. On top of her chronic bronchitis, she also had developed Barrett's esophagus as a result of her smoking and drinking aka self-medicating. I wonder if she had been on the proper medication and therapy management care that maybe her body would have been healthier after her fall, and she could have been here for longer. Instead after her accident she encountered every single problem that I had researched in regard to side effects from a spinal cord injury. Her bed sores were the evil little things that eventually would take her life, even though the care facility told us that bed sores were unlikely. A few weeks before my mother had finally passed I put my Nancy Drew knowledge to work and discovered what the nurse was talking about one morning after visiting my mother in the nursing home with my mother in law by my side. My mom at this point had developed a series of bed sores along the back side of her hips. At the time that she began to physically decompose in front of us her bed sores were well beyond a stageable level which meant that in nonmedical terms, you could shine a flashlight inside of her biggest wound at the surface of the skin and see tunnels spiraling in different directions as the wound had begun to hollow the inside of her body.

The week before my mom passed away we were briefed as a family in a small office by the hospice staff on exactly what to expect when my mom would physically die. Her ears and feet would lack the oxygen needed in order to circulate her blood flow, so her ears and feet were to turn a marbled purple when she was then pronounced dead. I was the first person to arrive at her hospice room after she left us. Gently closing her eyelids and telling her how loved she was I knew how hard she wanted to live under different circumstances, because deep down I know that I am just like my mother and if I were dying all I would want to know is that I was loved.

Two weeks before my mom passed away, we were told by the nursing home staff that my mother was nearing the end of her timeline and I felt like I was the only one who could hear them say this to us. My family had such hope, such god, so many family functions, so many charities and t-shirts, but when the numbing reality of existence settles in you can truly see through those rose-colored glasses that the fog has lifted and so has her spirit from her human shell. Sleeping beauty was not to wake again and I knew from the title what we were in for. I was screaming in our family meetings with rage and tears, but no one could hear me or rather they just chose not to. My signature was never on the paperwork. My voice was never heard. Sit down, shut up, let me talk, listen up. I will no longer be silent because I am just like my mother, and I will fight until my last breath to let you know that just as my mom did. I am thankful for the time I was given to be with my mother, and I forgive myself for not being the best daughter at times. I see her every morning when I look out my bathroom window after my painfully steamy morning shower, she sits as a bright red cardinal perched on a branch of the neighbor's tree. I see her face in a purple orb that radiates from a solar flare on my camera lens, she is every purple flower, she is every Thursday night spent inside and curled up on the couch binge watching garbage tv and eating garbage snacks, she is every holiday and every purposefully missed call. She is my mother, and I am her second born daughter. She gave me the gift of life and now I will give her life honor and love. My life has been the best adventure I've ever gone on and I cannot wait to see what comes next. Without the medication and team of experts I have taking care of me and my mental health I wouldn't be here to tell you this story plan and simple. This is my life, and my problems are not your problems but that doesn't mean that I or my life doesn't matter. Your life is yours and your problems are not my problems but that doesn't mean that you don't matter. Or maybe our problems are similar, and we are actually a lot alike in our journeys or perhaps none of this has been real and none of it matters and it's all just been in my head.

The very same month just a few weeks before my mother had her accident I did something I thought I would never have the courage to do. I tried stand-up comedy. I have always loved making people laugh, I love being the funniest person in the room. I once had someone sign my yearbook by saying, "Simone you are the funniest fucking person I have ever met, well funniest girl anyway." Girls can be funny too, you know? We can be fucking hilarious. We can crush it on stage and crush your sad, little, pee pee in the sheets. My first stand up performance was in Silver Spring, Maryland at what I thought was an open mic. No, it was an actual stand-up comedy show in a restaurant. I chugged a long island tea and power walked up the stairs with my husband, my dad, my stepmom, and a handful of friends. It was a "bringer show," which meant that I had to bring at least five people with me to the show to be able to go on stage. My mom opted to watch my kids and I promised I would take her to the next comedy show I was in. By the time I had my second comedy show I was newly knocked up and in no mood to be silly. It was still two weeks before she would fall and slowly decline but I broke my promise to her, and she did not accompany me to my second stand up gig. Instead, she was again at home with my kids. She was always pushing me to be who I wanted to be and do what I wanted to do, as long as she could come along with me every step of the way. I suppose I never realized that is what true parental support is. Loving your child and pushing them to be the best they can possibly be while maintaining their manors and humbleness in a cold, lonely world. If there is one thing I have learned from my mother it is how to love wholly even if it is with my little, black, heart.

Tight hugs and deep breaths
　　　- Simone Le Ann

Made in the USA
Middletown, DE
07 June 2024